Hebrews

The Superiority of Christ

_____

A Bible-Based Study
For Group and Individual Use
Leader's Guide Included

First Printing – October 2009
Lamplighters International
St. Louis Park, Minnesota USA 55416

Lamplighters International is a ministry that publishes Christ-centered, Bible-based teaching discipleship resources.

For additional information about the Lamplighters ministry resources contact:
Lamplighters International 6301 Wayzata Blvd, St. Louis Park, Minnesota USA 55416 or visit our web site at www.LamplightersUSA.org.

ISBN # 1-931372-23-3
Order # He-NK-SS

Contents

How to Use This Bible Study

What is Lamplighters?

Lamplighters International publishes Christ-centered, Bible-based resources for the glory of God, the edification of His people, and the salvation of the lost. The ministry offers a series of inductive discipleship resources and leadership training materials. Each Lamplighters Bible Study is a self-contained unit, but an integral part of the entire discipleship ministry. The companion Self-Study Edition booklet makes an excellent discipleship tool to help you lead another person through this study once you have completed all the lessons.

This study is comprised of fourteen individual lessons, although your Bible study group may prefer to do two lessons at a time for a seven-week format. When you have completed the entire study you will have a much greater understanding of a significant portion of God's Word, with new truths you can apply to your life.

How to Study a Lamplighters Lesson

A Lamplighters lesson begins with prayer, your Bible, the weekly lesson, and a sincere desire to learn more about God's Word. The questions are presented in a progressive sequence as you work through the study material. You should not use any Bible Commentaries and other Bible reference books until you have completed your weekly lesson and met with your class. When you approach the Bible lesson in this way you will have the opportunity to discover valuable spiritual insights from the Word of God.

To gain the most out of the Bible study, find a quiet place to complete your weekly lesson. Each lesson will take approximately thirty minutes to complete. You will likely spend more time on the first few lessons until you are familiar with the format, and our prayer is that each week will bring the discovery of important life principles.

The writing space within the weekly studies provides the opportunity for you to answer questions and to respond to what you have learned. Write the answers in your own words and include Scripture references where appropriate. This will help you personalize and commit to memory the truths you have learned. The answers to the questions will be found in the Scripture references at the questions or in the passages listed at the beginning of each lesson.

"*Do You Think*" Questions

Each weekly lesson has a few "*do you think*" questions designed to help you gain personal applications from the biblical truths you are learning. Make a special effort to answer these questions because they are designed to help you apply God's Word to your life. In the first lesson the "*do you think*" questions are placed in italic print for easy identification. If you are part of a study group, your insightful answers to these questions could be a great source of spiritual encouragement to others.

Personal Questions

Occasionally you will be asked to respond to personal questions that, if you are part of a study group, you may choose not to share with the others. However, be sure to answer these questions for your own benefit because they will help you compare your present level of spiritual maturity to the biblical principles presented in the lesson.

Leadership Training

Lamplighters International provides a variety of discipleship training for pastors, small group leaders, and individuals who are interested in learning how to disciple others. Visit our website for more information on discipleship workshops and seminars, as well as on-line e-training.

A Final Word

Throughout this study the masculine pronouns are often used in the generic sense to avoid awkward sentence construction. When the pronouns "he," "him," and "his" are used in reference to the Trinity (God the father, Jesus Christ, and the Holy Spirit), they always refer to the masculine gender.

This Lamplighters study is presented after many hours of careful preparation. It is our prayer that it will help you *"... grow in the grace and knowledge of our Lord and Savior Jesus Christ. To Him be the glory both now and forever. Amen"* (2 Pet. 3:18).

About the Author

John Alexander Stewart was raised near Winnipeg, Canada. He was drafted by the Pittsburgh Penguins (NHL) and played professional hockey for eight years. He was converted to Jesus Christ in 1977 and graduated from seminary in 1988. He served as a pastor for fifteen years, planting two Bible-believing churches and founding Lamplighters International. He currently serves as the executive director of Lamplighters International and continues to write and speak at conferences and in churches.

Introduction

Hebrews is written to Jewish Christians who were facing persecution from their countrymen and as a result, tempted to return to Judaism. The writer exhorts them **to go on to perfection** (Heb. 6:2) instead of returning to life under the Old Covenant—the Law God gave to the Israelites on Mount Sinai.

The book answers key questions about the believer's relationship to God found nowhere else in the Bible. *"What is my relationship as a Christian to the Old Testament Law of Moses?" "Do Christianity and Judaism, two of the three great world religions, teach basically the same thing?" and, "Did Christ's sacrifice on the cross pay the entire penalty for my sin forever, or is there something else I must do to be accepted by God?"* These life-changing questions are answered conclusively in Hebrews.

Hebrews is also a call to bold discipleship. The writer confronts the readers' spiritual complacency with the boldness of an Old Testament prophet. Five *solemn warnings* (see a brief explanation below) challenge Christians with the most sobering words of warning in the entire Bible. To the writer of Hebrews there can be no casual approach to following Jesus. You're either growing toward spiritual maturity, or you're already in a state of falling away from the Savior—a very perilous situation for any believer.

Recipients and Date

The title "The Epistle (or letter) to the Hebrews" was added later, but internal evidence strongly points to Jewish believers as the original recipients. Fifty-seven of the Hebrews' 303 verses are direct quotations from the Old Testament. An additional 152 verses (roughly 50% of the entire letter) make direct reference to the Old Testament. In addition, most of these quotations and references assume a familiarity with ancient Jewish religious life that strongly points to Jewish believers as the original recipients of the letter.

The Jerusalem Temple, built by King Herod and under construction during Jesus' day (John 2:19–20), was central to Jewish religious life during the middle first century (Acts 3). The temple was totally destroyed by the Romans in 70 AD. The writer would undoubtedly have used the destruction of the temple as a main argument for the Jewish Christians not to return to Judaism. This has led many conservative scholars to believe that the book of Hebrews was written about 65-70 A.D.

Theme and Purpose

The theme of the book is the superiority of Jesus Christ. The word "better" appears thirteen times in the book: Christ is *better* than angels (Heb. 1:4), offers a *better* hope (Heb. 7:19), a *better* covenant (Heb. 7:22), a *better* promise (Heb. 8:6), a *better* sacrifice (Heb. 9:23), a *better* inheritance (Heb. 10:34), and a *better* (heavenly) country (Heb. 11:16). Christians can also gain a *better* resurrection as faithful followers of Jesus (Heb. 11:35).

Hebrews was written to encourage Jewish Christians facing persecution to remain faithful to Christ and not return to Judaism. Many Jewish believers were being tempted to return to Judaism to avoid further persecution, while others had become spiritually apathetic (Heb. 5:12–14, 6:12). The writer said there is more to be gained by following Christ than would be lost if they returned to Judaism.

The Five Solemn Warnings

One of the distinguishing characteristics of Hebrews are the five solemn warnings (Heb. 2:1–4, 3:7–4:13, 5:12–6:8, 10:26-39, 12:25–29) and they warn believers about the perils of spiritual lethargy. The five solemn warnings are presented in a progressive manner as you move through Hebrews. In Hebrews 2:1–4, believers are warned about being *casual* in their walk with God. In Hebrews 3:7–4:13, believers are warned of being *confused* about believing God's promises. In Hebrews 5:12–6:8, believers are warned about being *complacent* about their spiritual growth. In Hebrews 10:26–39, believers are warned about being *calloused* (hardened) toward intentional sin in their lives. And finally, in Hebrews 12:25–29, believers are warned about becoming *closed-minded* to the voice of God.

1: God's Ultimate Revelation

Read: Hebrews 1:1–14; other references as given.

What do you value most in life? Is it family, happiness, money, position (career success, influence within your community or church), or personal achievement? What motivates you toward a relentless pursuit of your goal? What we value most, we will pursue most ardently.

The writer of Hebrews presents Jesus Christ's superior value with the hope of inspiring his readers to strive for spiritual maturity. In Hebrews chapter one, Jesus is presented as God's ultimate revelation to man and the express image of His person (Heb. 1:1–3). Then the writer demonstrates Christ's superior value to angels, and concludes this chapter with a summary statement about the ministry of angels to believers today.

Before you begin, ask God to reveal Himself through His Word and to give you grace to accept the truths you will be learning.

1. The book of Hebrews begins abruptly, without identifying the human writer. Throughout the centuries, conservative Bible scholars have suggested various authors for Hebrews, but in the end, most agree with the third century theologian, Origen, who said of the unknown author, *"God only knows the truth."*

   a. Why isn't it essential to know the human author of Hebrews—or any other book of the Bible (2 Tim. 3:16; 2 Peter 1:20–21)?

   b. How does the writer describe his letter (Heb. 13:22)?

2. The writer begins by making a specific point: God's primary means of communicating to His people in these last days (the time between the first and second comings of Christ) has changed. God spoke to the Old Testament Jewish forefathers at various (NIV—"many") times and in various ways (Heb. 1:1).

   a. List four distinct ways God communicated to His people in the Old Testament (Gen. 3:9–13, 31:24; Ezekiel 1:1; Dan. 2:17-23, Amos 3:7).

   b. What *do you think* is the meaning of the statement **God…has spoken to us by His Son** (Heb. 1:2)?

3. When the Bible uses the phrase "The word of the Lord came to…" or, "Thus says the Lord…," it means God is communicating new truth or revelation to man. However, when some Christians make the statement "God spoke to me" they often mean the Holy Spirit convicted or convinced them of a specific truth from God's Word. In light of Hebrews 1:2, *do you think* a Christian should make a statement like this?   Why?

4. List nine things the Bible says about Jesus Christ (include verse references) that make him unique and superior to anyone who ever lived, including angels (Heb. 1:2–4).

5. What *do you think* is meant by the phrase, **the express image of His person** (Heb. 1:3; NIV—"exact representation of his being") (John 14:8–11)?

6. After introducing Jesus Christ as God the Father's ultimate revelation to man (Heb. 1:1–3), the writer compares Jesus Christ to angels (Heb. 1:4–13) and then concludes the chapter with a statement about the current ministry of angels (Heb. 1:14). The Jews held angels in very high regard because God used them to deliver the Law to Moses (Acts 7:53). In Hebrews 1:5–14, the writer quotes seven Old Testament passages (five from the Psalms) to prove why Jesus is superior to angels. Use the verse divisions to identify five reasons for Christ's supremacy (Heb. 1:5; 6–7, 8-9, 10–12, 13–14).

7   *The Supremacy of Christ*

7.   The Bible teaches that Jesus Christ is the creator of the world (Heb. 1:2; John 1:3; Col. 1:16), but in Heb. 1:6 it says He was the firstborn. In what way(s) *do you think* Jesus Christ can be both the creator and the firstborn (Heb. 1:6)?

8.   Angelology, the study of angels both good and evil (demons), fascinates and confuses many Christians. Some believers prefer to deny the existence of the angelic world, while others seem obsessed with demonic activity to the point of spiritual paranoia. What do the following verses teach about angels (Matt. 13:36–42, 22:29–30; Luke 15:10, 20:34–36; 1 Peter 1:10–12; Rev. 7:11–12)?

9.   Many people, including some Christians, believe guardian angels watch over them. The idea that adults have guardian angels is loosely based on Jesus' own words: **Take heed that you do not despise one of these little ones, for I say to you that in heaven their angels always see the face of My Father who is in heaven** (Matt. 18:10).

    a.   Do you think it is right for a Christian to believe in having his own guardian angel?

        Why?

    b.   Angels are created beings who worship and serve God, and minister to believers (Heb. 1:14). List two possible ways Christians could be led astray by believing that angels are more than ministering spirits (Col. 2:18; Exodus 20:3).

2: Captain of Our Salvation

Read: Hebrews 2:1–18; other references as given.

Who runs your life—God, you, your schedule, your boss? Somebody does! That person is the one you most frequently look to for acceptance and approval. It is the individual or group you think is superior. For the Christian, it should be Jesus Christ.

In Hebrews chapter one, the writer used several Old Testament passages to prove Christ's superiority to angels. In Hebrews chapter two, the writer presents the first solemn warning (Heb. 2:1–4) and then poses a rhetorical question, *How can Jesus, who was a man, inherit an everlasting kingdom if the Scriptures teach man was made lower than the angels?"* (Heb. 2:7, a quotation from Psalm 104:4).

The answer to this question is simple, yet profound. Jesus the Christ—creator, sustainer, heir of all things, and express radiance of the Father on earth—became man only *temporarily* and suffered death to redeem mankind. Christ's incarnation (the time He spent on earth) is only a snapshot of His eternal existence.

Before you begin, ask God to reveal Himself through His Word and to give you the grace to accept the truths you will be learning.

1. In the first solemn warning (Heb. 2:1–4), the writer includes himself (v. 1, **we must**), indicating all believers are tempted to neglect their salvation. The Greek word for "must"—*dei*—carries the force of "it is binding" or "it is necessary." The word **therefore** in this first verse of chapter two connects the immediate passage (Heb. 2:1–4) to the preceding doctrinal passage (Heb. 1:5–14) and makes application to all Christians. Give two reasons why believers must not neglect their salvation (Heb. 2:1–3).

2. The writer reminds the Jewish readers that their forefathers neglected God's commands during the Exodus and experienced His punishment (Heb. 2:2; Acts 7:52–53). Next, the writer asks a riveting question, **how shall we escape if we neglect so great a salvation?** (Heb. 2:3).

    a. What will all believers (including us) not escape if they neglect their salvation (Heb. 2:2–3)?

    b. What are some indicators a believer is neglecting his salvation?

      c.   Based upon the indicators in the previous question, in what areas of your Christian life are you currently being tempted to neglect your salvation?

3.   If you are a Christian, are there areas in your life God wants you to be more spiritually alert?

      If you aren't absolutely sure you are a Christian, please read *The Final Exam* located in the back of this Bible Study book.

4.   The writer originally learned the gospel of salvation from the apostles and prophets who heard it directly from Jesus Christ (Heb. 2:3). How did God authenticate the apostles' and prophets' original message about Jesus Christ (Heb. 2:4)?

5.   It is Jesus Christ, not angels, who will rule the world to come (Heb. 2:5). The writer's introduction of Psalm 8, **But one testified in a certain place** (Heb. 2:6, NIV—"there is a place where someone has testified"), seems to indicate that the writer is not certain where the biblical reference is located (a comfort to believers who struggle to remember specific verse references). What important truth do you think this phrase teaches about the giving of God's revelation and the human agents He used?

6.   The writer of Hebrews quotes Psalm 8:4–8 (Heb. 2:6–8). In its original setting, Psalm 8 speaks about God's willingness to include man in His original creative plan. Some Bible commentators believe the writer uses Psalm 8:4-8 to reemphasize that God's original goal for man (to rule over His earthly creation, Gen. 1:28–30) will be restored eventually. Other Bible commentators interpret Heb. 2:6–8 as a reference to Christ who temporarily became a man to redeem mankind. Give at least two reasons why the second interpretation is likely the better choice (Heb. 2:5–8).

7.	At first glance, the last portion of Heb. 2:8 seems to contradict itself: **For in that He put all in subjection under him, He left nothing** *that is* **not put under him. But now we do not yet see all things put under him.** However, the first part of the verse makes a general statement about the *extent* of Christ's authority as God and Lord, and the second part addresses the present *exercise* of Jesus' rule on earth. Use the following verses in sequence to explain the present and future rule of Jesus Christ on earth (Matt. 28:18; John 19:10–11; Matt. 4:8–9, 6:8–13; Rev. 11:15, 12:10).

8.	Jesus was made a little lower than the angels during His incarnation and tasted death on the cross for everyone, but not everyone is saved (Heb. 2:9). Jesus became the **captain** (Greek—*archegos*: leader, originator, founder, pioneer) of a large number (many sons) of people who inherit salvation (Heb. 2:10).

a.	Hebrews 2:17 is the first time the writer introduces Jesus as a merciful and faithful High Priest—a theme that will dominate much of the latter part of Hebrews. The role and responsibilities of the Israelite high priest are presented extensively in the Old Testament (especially the books of Exodus and Leviticus). Describe Jesus' present ministry as High Priest on behalf of Christians (Heb. 2:17–18).

b.	Sometimes believers think they have sinned too badly for God to forgive them. What does the Bible teach about Christ and His ministry on their behalf that will help them claim His complete forgiveness (Heb. 2:16–18)?

3: Doubt in the Desert

Read: Hebrews 3:1–19; other references as given.

Jesus is superior to angels (Heb. 1, 2), but is He superior to Moses, Israel's greatest leader? *"That's impossible!"* every clear thinking Jew would answer. After all, didn't God choose Moses to deliver His people out of Egypt? And didn't God choose Moses to receive the law on Mount Sinai? Surely Jesus is not greater than Moses.

In Hebrews 3, the writer proves why Jesus is superior to Moses. To every orthodox Jew (including these Jewish believers) this idea would have been a staggering concept with profound ethical and religious implications. By saying that Jesus is superior to Moses, the writer inferred that Christianity is superior to Judaism—a point not easily missed.

Before you begin, ask God to reveal Himself through His Word and to give you the grace to accept the truths you will be learning.

1. The writer addresses the Jewish believers as **holy brethren, partakers of the heavenly calling** (Heb. 3:1; Greek—*adelphos hagioi:* holy brothers; NIV—"holy brothers, who share in the heavenly calling"). However, he chided them later in the book for being insensitive to God's Word (Heb. 5:11) and spiritually sluggish (Heb. 6:12). How could they be called holy brethren if this were true?

2. The Jewish believers are commanded to **consider Jesus** (Heb. 3:1, Greek—*katanoeo*, aorist imperative; NIV—"fix your thoughts on Jesus"). Since they were already believers, this command must mean something different than a need for salvation. What do you think a Christian must do to fulfill this important command?

3. The Bible says **Moses was indeed faithful in all his house as a servant** (Heb. 3:2) and his name appears in the believers' "hall of faith" (Heb. 11). But Moses killed an Egyptian (Exod. 2:11–12) and disobeyed God when he struck the rock twice in anger (Num. 20:11). What does the writer's summary statement of Moses' life teach about how God views a believer's life and his individual failures (Heb. 3:2)?

4. Moses was an incredible man of faith and an exceptional leader of God's people. He delivered the Israelites from Egyptian oppression and led Israel for forty years in the wilderness.

a. How were Moses and Jesus similar (Heb. 3:2)?

b. How is Jesus superior to Moses (Heb. 3:3–6)?

5. Hebrews 3:7 begins the second and longest *solemn warning* (Heb. 3:7–4:13) with a quotation from Psalm 95:7–11. This psalm is a call to genuine, God-honoring worship (verses 1–7a), followed by a warning to believers not to allow their hearts to become hardened to God's voice (verses 7b–11).

a. Both Hebrews 3:7–11 and Psalm 95:7b–11 refer to the same event in Israel's history. What specific historical situation is meant by **the rebellion** (Heb. 3:8) and the **day of trial in the wilderness** (Heb. 3:8, 16)?

b. God allowed all the Israelite people who left Egypt (adults aged twenty and older) to die before seeing the Promised Land, with the exception of Joshua and Caleb (cf. Num. 32:10–16). Name two other negative consequences the Israelites experienced *before* they died (Heb. 3:11, 17)?

6. Moses led the Israelites out of Egypt to Mount Sinai (also called Horeb, Lev. 26:46; Deut. 5:2) where God gave him the Law of God (Exod. 20ff; also called the Old Testament Law, the Law, the Law of Moses, the commandments).

a. The Israelites wandered in the wilderness for forty years before they died. How long should the journey have taken from Mount Sinai (Horeb) to the entrance of the Promised Land at Kadesh Barnea (the southern entrance to the Promised Land, Deut. 1:2-3)?

b. Like the ancient Israelites, many Christians delay their spiritual journey and forfeit God's peace. Which of the following sins are you allowing to hinder your spiritual progress: pride, laziness, sexual sin, covetousness, envy, unforgiveness, gossip, slander, covetousness, anger, hatred, drunkenness?

c. Is there any reason why you shouldn't stop doing this Bible Study, repent of your sin, accept God's forgiveness, and begin to grow again toward spiritual maturity?

7.   God judged the Israelites' rebellion during the Exodus by not allowing them to enter His **rest** (Heb. 3:11, 18, Greek—*kataphausin*). The word **rest** appears twice in Hebrews 3, but the concept of a *spiritual rest* dominates the next chapter. What two things did God's original promise of rest mean for the Israelites (Deut. 12:9–11a)?

8.   Hebrews 3:12 is one of the most conflictive verses in the entire Bible because it speaks of a Christian who possess an **evil** (NIV—"sinful") **heart of unbelief**. Like the Israelites, some Christians rebel against God and wander in their own spiritual wilderness of fear and doubt. Rather than taking regular steps of faith, they seem content to attend church, but live in passive rebellion to God and doubt His promises.

   a.   If a Christian doesn't trust God, he may become **hardened through the deceitfulness of sin** (Heb. 3:13). What do you think this means?

   b.   What two things should every believer undertake to not become hardened against God (Heb. 3:12–13)?

9.   The phrases **whose house we are if we hold fast the confidence and the rejoicing of the hope firm to the end** (Heb. 3:6) and **we have become partakers of Christ if we hold the beginning of our confidence steadfast to the end** (Heb. 3:14) appear to teach that the believer's eternal destiny is determined by his own spiritual efforts. Since eternal salvation is a result of God's grace and not man's good works (John 1:12; Titus 3:5, etc.) what do these two verses teach about genuine salvation?

4: Promise of God's Rest

Consider Jesus, not just what He has done for you, but who He is—His love, His holiness, His mercy, His power, His righteousness, and His authority over this world and your life. Think about all the precious and magnificent promises He has for you in His Word. Then think about the blessings and peace you'll miss if you let a sinful, unbelieving heart turn you away from the living God.

Hebrews chapters one and two verified that Jesus is superior to angels for they worship Him. Jesus is superior to Moses for He created him (Heb. 3:1-6). Next the writer recounted Israel's original failure to enter the Promised Land and how that generation didn't experience God's rest (Heb. 3:7-19).

In Hebrews four, the Israelites' failure to enter the Promised Land is used as an illustration to challenge believers not to miss a future *spiritual rest*. But what is this rest?

Before you begin, ask God to reveal Himself through His Word and to give you the grace to accept the truths you will be learning.

1. The writer uses the word **therefore** (Heb. 4:1) to link the preceding passage about Israel's failure in the wilderness (Heb. 3:7–19) with the verses to follow (Heb. 4:1–13) to help his readers learn from the Israelites' error.

    a. List three similarities between the rest God offered the ancient Israelites and the rest God offers all Christians (Heb. 3:7–11, 18–19, 4:1–2, 11).

    b. Why didn't the Israelites learn from Moses' spiritual instruction (Heb. 4:2)?

    c. Upon what condition do God's people of all ages experience His rest (Heb. 4:2)?

2. Hebrews three and four are excellent examples of the benefits of studying the Old Testament. The vivid illustration of the Israelites' failure to enter God's rest can be a powerful reminder of what Christians should not do. What other benefits can be gained from studying the Old Testament (Rom. 15:4; 1 Cor. 10:1–11)?

3. The word **rest** (Greek—*katapausis*) dominates Hebrews four, appearing nine times in Hebrews 4:1–11. Do you think the rest God offers Christians refers to salvation or something else (Heb. 4:1–11)?

    Why?

4. Many Christians talk about "resting in the Lord" and "waiting on God." Unfortunately, some of them misapply what the Bible teaches about God's rest and use phrases like these to mask laziness and indolence. What do you think is the difference between resting in the Lord (which is endorsed in Scripture) and laziness or slothfulness?

5. List four things a Christian must do to gain God's rest (Heb. 4:1, 3, 6, 9–11).

6. At first glance, Hebrews 4:12 seems to be a separate truth and totally unrelated to the previous passage. However, the word **for** (Greek—*gar*) strongly suggests Hebrews 4:12 is closely connected to the preceding passage. What do you think is the connection between the rest God offers and the living power of His Word?

7. In the Greek New Testament, the word **living** (Greek—*dzon*) appears first in the sentence to emphasize its importance. The literal translation is "Living, for the word of God *is...*"

    a. What do you think is meant by the statement **the word of God is living** (Heb. 4:12; 2 Tim 3:16)?

b. God's Word is also **powerful** (Greek—*energes:* energetic, active, productive). In what ways do you think God's Word is powerful, energetic, active, and productive?

c. God's Word is also **sharp** (Greek—*tomoteros:* sharp). In what way is God's Word penetrating and able to help you more than any other book ever written (Heb. 4:12)?

8. For Christians to experience God's rest, they must allow His Word to examine and purify their actions and motives. What else must God's people realize if they desire God's best for their lives (Heb. 4:13)?

9. Jesus is God's ultimate revelation to man: creator, sustainer, heir of all things, brightness of His glory, express image of His person, savior (Heb. 1:2–3), captain of our salvation (Heb. 2:10), merciful and faithful High Priest (Heb. 2:17), and builder and owner of all things (Heb. 3:4–6). Jesus is also described as a great High Priest (Heb. 4:14). Why is Jesus such a **great High Priest** (Heb. 4:14–16)?

 **5: *Apathy Alert***

Howard Hendricks, distinguished seminary professor and Bible teacher extraordinaire, says there are three essentials keys to spiritual growth—the word of God, faith or obedience to God's Word, and time. Unfortunately, too many Christians have disregarded spiritual growth and experienced the devastating consequences of spiritual lethargy.

In Hebrews five, you'll learn that God expects every Christian to become spiritually mature. The writer compares the office of the Jewish high priest to Jesus, (Heb. 5:1–10) and introduces the third "solemn warning" (Heb. 5:11–6:18)—a warning to every Christian to grow according to God's (not man's) anticipated timeline.

Before you begin, ask God to reveal Himself through His Word and to give you the grace to accept the truths you will be learning.

1. The office of Jewish high priest, only alluded to previously (Heb. 2:17–3:1 and Heb. 4:14–16), becomes the central focus of Hebrews chapters five through ten. This priestly office was originally established when Moses received the Law of God at Mount Sinai. God instructed Moses to appoint and consecrate his older brother Aaron to serve in this priestly role (Exod. 28:1, 29:1–37; Lev. 8). The high priest's primary function was to offer gifts and sacrifices to God to atone for the Israelites' sins.

    a. List four characteristics of the Jewish high priest (Heb. 5:1).

    b. What weakness did all high priests possess that made them compassionate toward those who came to sacrifice (Heb. 5:2, 3)?

2. a. The priestly role was the most well-known office within ancient Jewish religious life. What two other key religious positions did God ordain to serve the Jewish people (Jer. 18:18)?

    b. What were the main religious designations during the early New Testament era (Eph. 4:11, 1 Peter 5:1)?

3. In the Greek New Testament, the phrase **some as pastors and teachers** (Eph. 4:11) refers to the same person (literally an individual with the gift of pastor/teacher). The spiritual leader (elder, pastor/teacher, minister, etc.) of a church shepherds the people and teaches them the Word of God. What is the primary ministerial (not denominational) difference between a priest and an elder/pastor?

4. Under the Old Covenant, Judaism had two priestly offices: the high priest and the Levitical priesthood. The high priest offered sacrifices and gifts and interceded for the people. God called Moses' brother Aaron and his descendants to fulfill this priestly duty. The Levitical priests (named after the Israelite tribe of Levi) were also chosen by God to serve (Num. 3:5–9).

    a. At the time of the Exodus, all the firstborn male children and firstborn animals were consecrated to the Lord. Why was this done (Exod. 13:1, 11–15)?

    b. If the Jew's firstborn males were originally consecrated to the Lord, how did the Levites come to replace the firstborns as God's servants (Num. 3:12–13, 32, 39–48)?

    c. What was the Levites' primary ministerial responsibility (Num. 3:6–9)?

5. a. There are two distinct, priestly roles during the New Testament church age. Who serves as the believer's high priest, and who serve as the priests (Heb. 5:12, 9:11, 1 Peter 2:1–5)?

    b. Why don't New Testament Christians need an earthly (high) priest who intercedes for them (1 Tim. 2:5–6; Heb. 7:25, 8:1)?

6. Every Jew knew the high priest wasn't self-appointed. God instructed Moses to consecrate Aaron and his descendants for this priestly service. No doubt many Jewish believers questioned Jesus' qualifications to be a high priest. How could these Jewish Christians be certain that Christ was a legitimate high priest, and not a usurper who claimed the office for Himself (Heb. 5:5–6)?

7.   As High Priest, Jesus did not offer various animal sacrifices. What were three results of sacrifices He offered, including His own life (Heb. 5:7–9)?

8.   Jesus was ordained as a high priest **according to the order of Melchizedek** (Heb. 5:6, 10). Melchizedek is a little-known Old Testament figure mentioned eleven times in Scripture, twice in the OT (Gen. 14:18; Psalm 110:4) and nine times in Hebrews. He was unique in that he served as both a king and a priest (Gen. 14:18). What do you think is the writer's point of stating that Christ was a high priest according to Melchizedek and not according to the descendants of Aaron?

9.   The writer interrupted his instruction about Jesus' qualifications to be a high priest to introduce the third *solemn warning*. For the first time in the book, the writer exposes the spiritual problem of his readers.

   a.   What time is meant by the phrase **though by this time** (Heb. 5:12)?

   b.   What is meant by the **milk** and **solid food** (Heb. 5:12–13)?

   c.   List four negative results of their lack of spiritual development (Heb. 5:12–14).

   d.   If you have been a Christian for a while, which (if any) of these four negative characteristics are part of your spiritual life?

   If you are a new Christian, in what ways does this passage challenge you to become spiritually mature?

6: *It's Time to Grow Up*

Read: Hebrews 6:1–20; other references as given.

To many within the church today, spiritual growth is an option to be considered rather than a passion to be pursued. Tragically, countless Christians have experienced the devastating consequences of casual Christianity.

In this lesson, you will study one of the most sobering warnings for Christians in the entire New Testament (Heb. 5:12–6:8). This warning is not just meant to scare you—it is meant to inspire you to spiritual maturity, **to go on to perfection** (Heb. 6:1).

Before you begin, ask God to reveal Himself through His Word and to give you the grace to accept the truths you will be learning.

1. What two things did the writer exhort the Jewish believers to do to become spiritually mature (Heb. 6:1)?

2. a. What do you think are the **elementary *principles*** (NIV—"teachings") about Christ (Heb. 6:1–2)?

    b. In the historical setting of Hebrews, what were the religious **dead works** (Heb. 6:1)?

    c. If you are a Christian, are you engaged in religious *dead works* (perhaps as part of your religious background) that have no biblical basis and for which you will need to repent?

3. In Heb. 6:2, the word **baptisms** is plural, meaning there is more than one baptism to be experienced by the believer. However, in Paul's letter to the Ephesians, he writes, ***There is* one body and one Spirit, just as you were called in one hope of your calling; one Lord, one faith, one baptism** (Eph. 4:5).

    a. List the two baptisms mentioned in the New Testament and explain when they occur in a person's life (1 Cor. 12:13; Titus 3:5; Acts 8:35–38).

    b.   Why do you think Paul referred to these two baptisms as only one baptism (Eph. 4:4–5)?

4.   Hebrews 6:4–6 forms the heart of the third *solemn warning*. This much-debated passage has yielded various interpretations that are often known by the following designations: 1) The "non-believer" view: Those who fall away are not real believers. They profess to be Christians, but they are not really saved. 2) The "Arminian" view: Those who fall away are believers who lose their salvation and can never be saved again. 3) The "First Century" view: Those who fall away were Jewish believers who could fall away before the destruction of the Jerusalem temple. According to this view, the *falling away* cannot be repeated because the temple has been destroyed. 4) The "Spiritual Deception" view: Those who fall away are believers who enter such a state of advanced spiritual deception that other (committed) believers cannot restore them to repentance (not salvation). They enter the arena of God's personal chastisement.

    a.   List the five-fold description of those who could fall away from the Lord (Heb. 6:4–5).

    b.   Based upon these five spiritual characteristics of those who fall away, do you think they are believers or non-believers (Heb. 6:4–6)?

    Why?

    c.   What are three results of their spiritual defection (Heb. 6:6)?

5.   The first key to interpreting this difficult passage is correctly indentifying those who fall away (believers or non-believers). The second key is a careful examination of Hebrews 6:6.

    a.   Is the passage stating that those who fall away can never be renewed again to repentance, or is it stating that it's impossible for someone else to renew those who have fallen away (Heb. 6:4–6)?

    b.   Who isn't able to renew those who have fallen away?

    c.   What is the main point of the third *solemn warning*?

6. The writer uses a familiar picture of the burning of a weed-infested field to emphasize God's lordship over the Christian's life and His expectations of spiritual fruitfulness (Heb. 6:7–8). If a parcel of land produces a useful crop, it's blessed by Him. What happens if the same parcel of ground yields only weeds (thorns and briars, Heb. 6:8)?

7. Hebrews 6:7–8 has been used by some interpreters to prove that believers who fall away from the Lord lose their salvation and perish in hell. However, a biblical illustration, like a parable, usually teaches a single truth.

   a. Do you think it is the ground, or the weedy thorns and briers (in the believer's case, sin and unfruitful works), that is being rejected and ready to be burned (cf. 1 Cor. 3:11–15)?

   b. What happens to a piece of land that is overgrown with weeds (thorns and briars) once a fire has passed over it?

8. The writer gave the Jewish believers strong words of warning, hoping they wouldn't continue to fall away from the Lord (Heb. 9–12). He assured them that God promises were still true even though they were experiencing testing. He used Abraham, a notable OT figure, as an example of one who received a promise from God (Heb. 6:13–14), was tested, persevered in faith, and finally received the fulfillment of God's original promise (Heb. 6:15).

   a. Christians often doubt God's promises, even though they know the promises are true. Name at least one of God's promises you know is true, but which you still struggle to believe on a daily basis.

   b. What are the two immutable (unchangeable) things that assure believers that God will fulfill all His promises (Heb. 6:17–18)?

   c. In the English language, hope is a present desire of an anticipated future possibility. In the Greek language, however, the word for **hope** (Greek—*elpis*) refers to a *present assurance of certain future event*. How should knowing the Greek definition for hope affect the believer's present confidence in God's future promises (Heb. 6:18–20)?

7: Mysterious Melchizedek

Every day millions of people attempt to connect with God through godless means. Some travel hundreds of miles hoping to cleanse their sin-stained souls in a remote river. Some adopt ascetic lifestyles, even denying themselves basic necessities, to atone for their sins and those of their forefathers. Others bow before man-made idols, offering ritualistic prayers to lifeless images of gold, silver, or wood. Still others attempt to find a divine spark within themselves through transcendental meditation, spirit guides, or other mystical experiences.

In Hebrews seven, the writer shows why all attempts to connect with God apart from Christ are imperfect and unprofitable. Christ's superiority to the Levitical priesthood is presented deductively (Heb. 7:1–10) and practically (Heb. 7:11–19). The chapter ends with several powerful statements about Christ's eternal work as High Priest and Savior (Heb. 7:20–28).

Before you begin, ask God to reveal Himself through His Word and to give you the grace to accept the truths you will be learning.

1. In Hebrews seven, the writer returns to his previous argument (Heb. 5:1–10) that Jesus is a superior high priest because he was ordained by God the Father as a priest according to a superior priestly line—**the order of Melchizedek** (Heb. 5:6, 10).

   a. Melchizedek is a little-known figure whose story occupies only four verses in the Old Testament. What does the Bible teach us about this mysterious individual (Gen. 14:18–20; Psalm 110:4; Heb. 7:1–3)?

   b. What two positions did Melchizedek hold (Heb. 7:2)?

2. The phrase **without father, without mother, without genealogy, having neither beginning of days nor end of life** (Heb. 7:3) seems bewildering. The wording has led some commentators to believe Melchizedek was an angelic figure or a pre-incarnate appearance of Christ.

   a. The best commentary on the Bible is the Bible itself. To interpret a difficult verse, examine the immediate passage for clues to help you understand the verse. What does the immediate passage say about Melchizedek that helps reveal his true identity (Heb. 7:1–10)?

    b.   What do you think is the meant by the phase **without father, without mother, without genealogy, having neither beginning of days nor end of life** (Heb. 7:3)?

3.   It is often tempting to assign a hidden, spiritual meaning to a difficult verse, even though the interpretation isn't supported by Scripture. When you study the Bible, do you accept the usual meaning of the words and study the immediate context for interpretative clues, or do you sometimes look for a *hidden* meaning that isn't supported by Scripture?

4.   The writer's review of the brief encounter between Abraham and Melchizedek is more than a Jewish history lesson. It provides the basis for a two-fold deductive argument that ultimately proves Christ's superiority as a priest **according to the order of Melchizedek**.

    a.   In Hebrew history, no one was more important than Abraham, the father of Jewish people. What is the first argument to prove the importance of the Melchizedekian order of priests (and Christ's priesthood) (Heb. 7:1–4)?

    b.   We need to understand Abraham's family lineage to understand the second argument. Abraham was the father of Isaac; Isaac was the father of Jacob; and Jacob was the father of Levi and his eleven brothers (Gen. 29:31–30:24). What is the writer's second point of his argument to show the superiority of the Melchizedekian priesthood and Jesus Christ (Heb. 7:5–10)?

5.   But wait! Jesus was also a descendent of Abraham through Jacob's fourth son, Judah (Matt. 1:1–17). Since every Jew would know this, what did Jesus say about his true heritage that excluded Him from this argument, even though he was a direct descendant of Abraham (John 8:54–58)?

6.   In Hebrews 7:1–10, the writer showed the *superiority* of the Melchizedekian priesthood to the Levitical priesthood. In Hebrews 7:11–19, the writer shows why

Christ's priesthood *supersedes* the Levitical priesthood. What argument does the writer present to prove the imperfection of the Levitical priesthood (Heb. 7:11)?

7. If the establishment of a second priestly line by God proves the first one (the Levitical priesthood) was imperfect, what also must be changed (Heb. 7:12–14)?

8. In Hebrews 7:15, the phrase **in the likeness of Melchizedek, there arises another priest** (NIV—"another priest like Melchizedek appears") refers to Jesus Christ. What are the similarities between Melchizedek and Jesus (Heb. 7:1–2, 17; Mark 15:26)?

9. Fill out the chart below to compare the differences between the Levitical priesthood and Christ's priesthood.

	Levitical Priesthood		Christ's Priesthood	
a. Priestly tribe	_____	(Heb. 7:11)	_____	(Heb. 7:14)
b. Ability to redeem	_____	(Heb. 7:19)	_____	(Heb. 7:25)
c. Number of Priests	_____	(Heb. 7:23)	_____	(Heb. 7:24)
d. Priest's character	_____	(Heb. 7:27–28)	_____	(Heb. 7:26)
e. Number of offerings	_____	(Heb. 7:27)	_____	(Heb. 7:27)

8: The New and Living Way to God

For the past two thousand years, the church has often done a poor job of representing Christ to the world. We have supplanted God's truth with man-made traditions and called it devotion (Mark 7:5–13). We have over-emphasized God's love, glossing over sin and calling it grace. We have confused mysticism with faith and called it higher spirituality. We have added our personal convictions to the fundamentals of the faith and judged others by false standards that God denounces (Rom. 14:1–13). We have misrepresented Christ, misused our God-ordained authority, and misunderstood the gospel. In spite of all this, our sovereign God continues to save the lost and sanctify the redeemed.

In Hebrews eight, you'll learn that theological confusion isn't the exclusive property of the New Testament church. You will learn that the Jews misunderstood the *purpose* and the lack of *permanence* of the Old Covenant—the Law God gave to Moses for Israel on Mount Sinai. And you will learn why and how the Old Covenant Law of Moses was replaced by a New Covenant.

Before you begin, ask God to reveal Himself through His Word and to give you the grace to accept the truths you will be learning.

1. In Hebrews five, the writer began a lengthy explanation of Christ's superiority as high priest that continues into Hebrews eight and beyond. Although the writer's argument wasn't complete, he made a summary statement (Greek—*kephalaion:* the chief point, sum, synopsis) in Hebrews 8:1.

    a. What is this main point the Jewish readers needed to understand (Heb. 8:1)?

    b. To whom does the word "we" refer to in the phrase **We have such a High Priest, who is seated at the right hand of the throne of the Majesty in the heavens** (Heb. 8:1)?

2. On Mount Sinai, God gave Moses the Law—a comprehensive legal and moral code to govern the infant nation of Israel (Exod. 20ff.). God also gave Moses a detailed plan to build a portable worship facility called the **tabernacle** (Hebrew—*miskan:* sanctuary, dwelling place, or tent of meeting, Exod. 25–31, 35–40). The entire tabernacle was comprised of a small enclosed tent covered with animal skins and linen cloth, and a larger open outer court surrounded by a fence of hanging curtains (Exod. 27:9-19). The **tent of meeting** was divided into two rooms separated by a single curtain. The first room, called the Holy Place, contained three items—a lampstand, a table with the Bread of Presence, and the Incense Altar on it. The second room, called the Most

Holy Place or Holy of Holies, contained the Arc of the Covenant or Mercy Seat (a small rectangular box), that held the two tablets Moses received from God, a sample of manna from the wilderness, and Aaron's staff.

a. What are the similarities between the Old Testament form of worship in the tabernacle and Jesus' ministry as High Priest in the **true tabernacle** of heaven (Heb. 8:1–3)?

b. List four important differences between Old Testament worship in the tabernacle and Jesus' ministry as high priest in the **true tabernacle** (Heb. 8:1–3, 10:11)?

3. The various items placed in the tabernacle may seem strange to us, but they were important reminders to the Jews of God's holiness, presence, and miraculous provision. For New Testament believers, the Old Testament form of worship serves as a **copy and shadow** of what is in heaven (Heb. 8:5). What do you think this means?

4. Jesus is a *better* high priest and He is the minister of a *better* covenant based upon *better* promises (Heb. 7:22, 8:6). List several promises available to those who accept Him as Savior and Lord (Heb. 2:14–15, 4:9, 6:19–20, 7:25–27)

5. In Hebrews 8:6–13, the writer compares the Old Covenant God made with Israel at Mount Sinai with the New Covenant. There are eight major biblical covenants in the Bible—six are unconditional and two are conditional. God is obligated to fulfill the unconditional covenants regardless of man's actions (Adamic—Gen. 3:16–19, Noahic—Gen. 9:1–18, Abrahamic—Gen. 12:1–4, 13:14–17, 15:1–7, 17:1–8, Palestinian—Deut. 30:1–10, Davidic—2 Sam. 7:4–16, New Covenant—Jer. 31:31–34). In the two conditional covenants, God is obligated to fulfill His promise(s) as long as specific human requirements are met (Edenic—Gen. 1:26–31, 2:16–17, Mosaic—Exod. 20:1-31:18).

a.   What are some other names for the old (Mosaic) covenant (Heb. 8:7; 2 Cor. 3:7, 9)?

b.   Why was the Old Covenant (also called the Law, the Law of God or the Law of Moses) called a **ministry of death** or a **ministry of condemnation** (Rom. 7:7–10)?

6.   Some Christians believe the Law of Moses is an example of a faulty legal code, one that failed and had to be replaced. However, the Apostle Paul said the law is **holy, just,** and **good** (Rom. 7:12). What purpose (if any) does the Law of Moses still fulfill (Rom. 7:7-12; Gal. 3:19–25)?

7.   The Prophet Jeremiah prophesied about a day when God would enter into a New Covenant with Israel (Jer. 31:31–34; Heb. 8:8, the house of Israel and the house of Judah). Although Christians experience many of the blessings of the New Covenant (1 Cor. 11:25; 2 Cor. 3:6), its ultimate fulfillment will occur in the future millennial kingdom (Rev.20:4–6) when Christ rules on earth and His command to make disciples has ceased (Matt. 28:18–20).

a.   When was the New Covenant initiated (Matt. 26:26–30, 27:51)?

b.   The Bible says the first covenant is **becoming obsolete, growing old,** and **vanishing away** (Heb. 8:13). If the Old Covenant is holy, just, and good (Rom. 7:12) and is still the tutor or schoolmaster (NIV—"put in charge") that brings men to Christ (Gal. 3:24), in what ways do you think it is obsolete, growing old, and ready to vanish (Heb. 8:13)?

9: The New Covenant

The Bible says it is possible to know for certain you'll go to heaven when you die. The Apostle John wrote **These things I have written to you who believe in the name of the Son of God, that you may <u>know</u> that you have eternal life** (1 John 5:13). You don't have to live in doubt and fear! God has provided the only way for you to be saved and to have complete assurance of your acceptance into heaven, but there is no second chance (Heb. 9:27).

Hebrews nine contrasts Christ's complete sufficiency to redeem man with man's insufficiency to redeem himself. Before you begin, ask God to reveal Himself through His Word and to give you the grace to accept the truths you will be learning.

1. Hebrews 9:1–5 provides a general description of the items found in the Old Testament tabernacle's Holy Place (Heb. 9:2, 6) and the Holiest of All (Heb. 9:3–5, 7). The writer's objective was to establish the setting within the tabernacle before explaining the priestly duties and their comparison to Christ.

    a. What articles were located in the Holy Place (Heb. 9:2)?

    b. What was in the Holiest of All (Heb. 9:4–5)?

2. The items in the sanctuary (tent of meeting) reminded the Israelites' of God's holiness, His miraculous delivery of His people from Egypt, His willingness to dwell among the people (the tabernacle was located in the middle of the camp), and their need for forgiveness. What two things were taught by the restrictive access to the Holiest of All and the priest's recurring offerings (Heb. 9:8, 9)?

3. The high priest entered into the Holiest of All once a year on the Day of Atonement (Heb. 9:7; Lev. 16:29–34). The Hebrew designation for this day is *Yom Kippur,* and it is held on the 10th day of the seventh month of the Jewish calendar (*Tishri*— October/November). As part of the high priest's preparations, he sacrificed a young bull as a sin offering for the sins he and his family had committed and he sacrificed a ram as a burnt offering on the incense altar (Lev. 16:3). The incense altar was located in the tabernacle's outer court, between the main entrance and the tent of meeting.

    a. Besides the offering of the young bull and the ram, the high priest offered two young goats—one that was sacrificed to the Lord and the other called the **scapegoat** (Hebrew—*azazel*) that was released live into the wilderness (Lev.

16:10). What did the high priest do before he released the **scapegoat** (Lev. 16:20–22)?

b.   What is the spiritual significance of the high priest placing both hands on the head of the scapegoat and confessing the nation's sins before the goat was released (Lev. 16:8-10, 20–22)?

4.   List at least three similarities between the Old Testament picture of the scapegoat's release and Jesus Christ's crucifixion (John 19:16–17; 1 Peter 2:24).

5.   The scapegoat was released into the wildness and bore the sins of the people. The scapegoat pre-figured Jesus Christ who was also led away (outside Jerusalem) to Golgotha to bear the sins of the world (John 19:16–17). The Bible takes the illustration one step further when it says **Therefore let us go forth to Him, outside the camp—** an obvious reference to the Jews' Old Testament wilderness wanderings.

a.   What do you think it means to **go forth to Him, outside the camp** (Heb. 13:13)?

b.   What do you think it means to **go forth to Him, outside the camp, bearing His reproach** (Heb. 13:13)?

c.   If you are a Christian, how are you fulfilling this important command (Heb 13:13–14)?

6.   List four important differences between Old Testament offerings and Jesus' sacrifice (Heb. 9:9–15).

7. When an individual trusts Christ as his personal Savior, his conscience is cleansed and he understands that good works don't save him (Heb. 9:14). Man's conscience is a gift from God, and it is one of the things that distinguishes him from the animal kingdom. List six kinds of consciences mentioned in the Bible (Acts 23:1; 1 Cor. 8:7; 1 Tim. 3:9, 4:2; Titus 1:15; Heb. 9:14, 10:22; include verse references for each).

8. The Greek word for covenant (*diatithemia*) can also be translated **testament** (Heb. 9:16). The writer uses this meaning of *diatithemia* to show that Jesus had to die to fully initiate the New Covenant stipulations (Heb. 9:16–22). Theories about Jesus' death and questions about the location of His body began to circulate shortly after His death (Matt. 28:11–15).

   a. In the Apostle Peter's sermon on the day of Pentecost, he answers three rhetorical questions, including one about Christ's death: *"If Jesus was really God, how could men kill him?"* (Acts 2:22–28); *"If Jesus rose from the dead where is He now?"* (Acts 2:29–35); and, *"If Jesus is really in heaven, what is His present status?"* (Acts 2:36). Give three reasons why Jesus' blood had to be shed (Heb. 9:16–28).

   b. What words and phrases are used to prove that Christ's sacrifice was a once-for-all sacrifice—sufficient to pay the complete penalty for man's sin (Heb. 9:25–28)?

   c. Beliefs regarding the hereafter differ greatly. Major eastern religions such as Hinduism (New Age), Buddhism, and Sikhism believe in endless reincarnation based upon "works." Islam teaches that an individual spends eternity in jannat (Paradise) or jahannam (Hell) also based on "works." Atheism teaches annihilation, and Jehovah Witnesses teach *soul sleep* with a resurrection available for 144,000 righteous souls—also based on "works." What will happen to all men when they die (Heb. 9:27)?

10: One Sacrifice for All Time

When an individual says he is born again (redeemed, saved) and has complete assurance of salvation, his statement may appear boastful or prideful. Is he boasting about his own religious devotion, or has he accepted Christ's free gift of salvation and embraced God's invitation to be assured of his eternal destiny?

In Hebrews ten, you'll learn Christ's death on the cross was a once-for-all sacrifice completing the work of salvation. You'll also learn that God invites those who are truly redeemed to fully embrace His offer of **full assurance of faith** (Heb. 10:22–23). This assurance is based upon God's character and promises, not on man's continuing good works.

Before you begin, ask God to reveal Himself through His Word and to give you the grace to accept the truths you will be learning.

1.   How is the Old Testament Law of Moses described (Heb. 10:1)?

2.   a.   The Greek word for **shadow** (*skia*) signifies an outline or shadow cast by an object. In what ways is the Law of Moses, specifically the tabernacle worship, a shadow of **the good things to come** (Heb. 10:1, NIV—"the good things that are coming")?

     b.   What are **the good things to come** (Heb. 9:12–15)?

     c.   A shadow reflects the image's reality, but there is always some distortion or imperfection in the reflection. The Greek word for image (*eikon*) means more of an exact representation. John Calvin, the great French theologian, believed the word "shadow" reflected an artist's outline sketch, and the word "image" reflected the finished portrait. What aspect of Jesus' sacrifice doesn't the Old Testament Law's sacrificial system reflect accurately (Heb. 10:1–4)?

3.   Under the Old (Mosaic) Covenant, the people brought gifts and sacrifices to the priests who offered them to God for sins committed (Lev. 1:1–7:36, 16:1–34). The Bible says, **So the priest shall make atonement for his sin that he has committed, and it shall be forgiven him (Lev. 4:35).**

     a.   If the Old Testament Law states explicitly that the worshippers' sins were forgiven when the sacrifice was offered (Lev. 4:20, 26, 35), what is the meaning of the statement **For *it is* not possible that the blood of bulls and goats could take away sins** (Heb. 10:4)?

b.   What are the main differences between the Old Testament sacrifices and Jesus' sacrifice (Heb 10:1–10)?

4.   The Bible says **And every priest stands ministering daily and offering repeatedly the same sacrifices, which can never take away sins** (Heb. 10:11). What phrases are used to describe the effectiveness of Christ's sacrifice (Heb. 10:12–18)?

5.   Various Christian religious groups often present images of Jesus Christ that emphasize a particular aspect of His life and work (with a child to reflect His gentleness or humility, on the cross to picture His suffering, etc.). Where is Jesus Christ presently, and what does this signify (Heb. 10:12, 18)?

6.   The study of God's Word is never meant to be a religious exercise void of personal life application. Of the 394 occurrences of the word **therefore** in the New Testament, a majority of them exhort believers to make an immediate, direct application to their lives.

a.   What amazing privilege has God given Jewish and non-Jewish believers as a result of Jesus' sacrifice (Heb. 10:19)?

b.   What supernatural thing happened when Christ was crucified, giving all believers direct access to God (Mark 15:33–39)?

7.   What three acts of devotion are believers commanded to do to demonstrate their new access to God (Heb. 10:22–24, all beginning with the words "Let us ...")?

8.   Some believers are inconsistent in both church attendance and fellowship with other believers. Christians are warned about **not forsaking the assembling of ourselves together** (Heb. 10:25). Sometimes believers think attending church is strictly about them (Are my needs being met? Do I like the pastor's preaching, worship, etc?). Why

should every believer seek genuine worship and fellowship with other Christians (Heb. 10:24)?

9. Hebrews 10:26–31 form the fourth (and most sobering) of the five *solemn warnings*. Each warning addresses the believer's relationship to God and His Word. The first solemn warning exhorts believers not to be <u>casual</u> about their salvation (Heb 2:1–4). The second solemn warning exhorts believers not to be <u>carnal</u> and forfeit God's promises (Heb. 3:7–4:13). The third solemn warning exhorts believers not to be <u>complacent</u> about their spiritual growth (Heb. 5:12–6:8). The fourth solemn warning exhorts believers not to be <u>callous</u> about sin in their lives (Heb. 10:26–31).

    a. What will be the divine consequences if we (believers) **sin willfully** (NIV— "deliberately keep on sinning") **after we have received the knowledge of the truth** (Heb. 10:26–27)?

    b. If a believer deliberately sins after he has received the knowledge of the truth, why do you think there is no longer a sacrifice for his sins (Heb. 10:26)?

    c. If we deliberately keep on sinning after receiving the knowledge of the truth, the Bible says we are treating the blood of the covenant as a common (NIV— "unholy") thing and insulting the Spirit of grace (Heb. 10:29). What do you think this means?

    d. What promise is given to believers who deliberately keep on sinning after receiving the knowledge of the truth (Heb. 10:30–31)?

10. Even though the writer has solemnly warned these Jewish believers, he was mindful of the great trials and persecutions they endured (Heb. 10:32–34) and was hopeful they would renew their devotion to follow Christ. What two things did he exhort them to do (Heb. 10:35–39)?

11: The Definition of Faith

In Hebrews eleven, the writer changes from teaching about the superiority of Christ to the importance of living by faith. Did the writer simply exhaust the theological subject of Christ's superior priesthood and suddenly move to another relevant, but unrelated, topic? Hebrews 10:32–39 provides an important link between the previous section (chapters 1–10) and the remainder of the book (chapters 11–13). The Jewish believers had started well (Heb. 10:32–34), but they had stopped living by faith. They'd become impatient and discouraged as they waited for God to fulfill His promises (Heb. 10:35–36).

In Hebrews eleven, the writer explains that living by faith isn't optional for true believers. Beginning with Adam's son Abel, then Enoch and Noah (Heb. 11:1–7), the writer provides ample evidence that living by faith is pleasing to God and changes the world. In this lesson you'll learn what faith is, what it isn't, and why it's important for Christians to learn to live by faith.

Before you begin, ask God to reveal Himself through His Word and to give you the grace to accept the truths you will be learning.

1. Hebrews eleven is commonly known as the believer's "hall of faith" because it chronicles several Old Testament saints. Eighteen of the chapter's 40 verses begin with the words **By faith** (Greek—*pistie*). The frequency of this phrase and its location in the original text (standing first in the Greek) highlights the importance of faith and proves it is the basis of all life-changing, God-honoring conduct.

    a. What is your definition of faith? (Note: Please give a general definition, not necessarily one related to a belief in God.)

    b. In Hebrews 10:22, the writer encouraged the Jewish believers to **draw near with a true heart in full assurance of faith.** What do you think is the difference between a general faith in God and a saving faith with full assurance?

2. Many people never analyze their faith in God. They believe it's enough to acknowledge the existence of a supreme being or higher power. To them it's about having faith (in the supernatural, a person, object, force, power, guiding principle)—something to take their minds off themselves and their problems and provide assurance that things happen for the best.

a. List three individuals or groups who believed in God in a general sense, but whose belief in God fell short of His standard of acceptance (Matt. 7:21–23; John 8:37–44; James 2:19).

b. In each of the 18 occurrences of the phrase **By faith** in Hebrews eleven, there is an ensuing action (By faith [person's name] offered/pleased/prepared/obeyed, etc.). A genuine faith in God always produces a God-honoring life change. What did the Apostle Paul encourage the people in the Corinthian church to do when their religious conduct didn't reflect a genuine faith in God (2 Cor. 13:5)?

c. Are you absolutely certain you possess more than a general belief in God? Have you examined your faith in God according to the Bible? Does your faith in God pass the test mentioned in 2 Cor. 13:5, so that you can stand before God with confidence in the final judgment?　　　If not, please read *The Final Exam* located in the back of this Bible Study.

3. Faith is trusting God and doing what He has commanded regardless of the circumstances or the consequences. Faith is concerned with scriptural facts—not speculations or impressions. George Mueller, a great man of faith, said *"It is not impressions, strong or weak, which make the difference. We have to do with the written Word and not ourselves or our impressions."*

a. Some Christians misinterpret the phrases **things hoped for** and **things not seen** (Heb. 11:1). They believe faith is a present expectation of a future *possibility*. In lesson six, you learned the Greek word for **hope** means a present assurance of a *certain future event*. With that in mind, give an accurate definition of the meaning of biblical faith.

b. What two things must be present in a believer's life if he expects to grow in faith (Rom. 10:17; Heb. 4:2)?

4. Many Christians believe that knowing God and comprehending the origin of creation must start with reason and then add faith. Their argument goes something like this: A complex (or intelligent) world must have an intelligent "maker" (human reason). That must mean there must be an intelligent maker/creator, but He is known only by faith (the "reason-to-faith" progression).

a.   Non-Christians often perceive Christians as irrational, illogical mystics who cast away all reason and logic. Unfortunately, their perception is often accurate. What words or phrases does the Bible use to demonstrate the interrelatedness of genuine faith and human reason (Acts 16:9–11; Heb. 11:3)?

b.   The Bible says **by faith we understand** (Heb. 11:3), not "by reason we comprehend." Why must faith (not human reason or speculation) be the foundational principle to understanding divine creation and other important spiritual truths (1 Cor. 2:11–14; 2 Cor. 4:4)?

5.   Living by faith should be the normal expression of the believer's trust and devotion to God. If a Christian is motivated by unholy fear, guilt, or pride, he won't be able to live by faith. How did faith in God influence the following individuals' actions:

a.   Abel (Heb. 11:4)?

b.   Enoch (Heb. 11:5)?

c.   Noah (Heb. 11:7)?

d.   Abraham (Heb. 11:8–9)?

e.   Sarah (Heb. 11:11)?

6.   a.   What does the Bible say about the importance of living by faith (Heb. 11:6)?

b.   What did Jesus say in the parable of the unjust judge about genuine faith (Luke 18:1–8)?

12: Triumph of Faith

Read: Hebrews 11:13–40; other references as given.

Evidence that the church at large is confused about faith is seen in the myriad of different teachings on the subject. Many faith healers preach that all sickness can be healed if individuals only have enough faith. The Word of Faith churches (also called Positive Confession) believe individuals who speak the Word of God out loud will receive whatever they confess. The Prosperity Gospel or Health-Wealth movement encourages followers to exercise their faith and claim their share of God's material abundance. Others believe faith is essentially something extra-biblical—a divine revelation from God that often goes beyond what the Bible teaches.

In this lesson, you'll learn that faith is trusting God even though the deepest desires of your heart aren't realized. Now before you begin, ask God to reveal Himself through His Word and to give you the grace to accept the truths you will be learning.

1.   Some Christians view faith as holding on in prayer until God answers. But what about the person who believes without wavering and their prayers are not realized? Did they not have enough faith? Did God fail them?

   a.   How does the Bible describe the faithful believers who died before they received the realization of God's promises (Heb. 11:13)?

   b.   There is an excellent three-fold definition of biblical faith in Hebrews 11:13. What are the three characteristics of genuine faith?

2.   What do Christians who live by faith declare to the world (Heb. 11:14)?

3.   The well-known expression, "Your home is where your heart is," can be applied to the believer regarding how he sees this world and the next. If a Christian is not willing to live by faith, he'll soon abandon the dynamic relationship He has with Christ and return to formalistic religion (like the Jewish believers to whom the letter was written).

   a.   What will be a believer's perspective if he learns to live by faith (Heb. 11:15–16)?

   b.   Does this world feel like home, and heaven like a distant illusion, or does heaven feel like your real home, and this world seem about to vanish?

4. Living by faith is also the key to overcoming the world. First John 5:4 says **For whatever is born of God overcomes the world. And this is the victory that has overcome the world—our faith.** What does it mean to overcome the world, and how is faith the key to this victory?

5. Abraham is an excellent example of a believer who lived by faith and overcame the world. His story provides a clear portrait of the four stages every believer experiences as they consistently live by faith (Heb. 11:17). The four stages are: 1. Promise. 2. Trial. 3. Crisis of faith. 4. Decision. If the believer lives by faith and trusts God, he is blessed. If not, he experiences defeat, but God continues his sanctification.

    a. What *promise* did God give Abraham (stage one, Heb. 11:18; Gen. 15:1–6)?

    b. What was Abraham's trial (stage two, Gen. 22:1–2)?

    c. What was Abraham's *crisis* of faith (stage three)?

    d. How do we know Abraham made a *decision* (stage four) to trust God and live by faith (Gen. 22:3–10)?

    e. God rewarded Abraham for living by faith. How did Abraham win the victory during his *crisis of faith* (Gen. 22:5, 8; Heb. 11:19)?

6. Promise, trial, crisis of faith, decision, blessing or defeat—these are the stages every believer goes through in the faith-building process. Identify one of God's promises that you have struggled to apply. How could you apply this faith-building process to your life?

7. Faith is not presumptuously claiming deliverance over every earthly trial. It is trusting God regardless of the earthly outcome. What important spiritual truths can we learn from Shadrach, Meshach, and Abed-Nego's answer to Nebuchadnezzar about God's ability and willingness to deliver His people from their trials (Dan. 3:13–18)?

8. The writer of Hebrews continues to present an impressive list of well-known Jews who lived by faith—Abel, Enoch, Noah, Abraham, Sarah, Isaac, Jacob, Joseph (Heb. 11:1–22). His point: Living by faith should be the norm for God's people, not the exception.

    a. Moses' parents, Amran and Jochebed (Exod. 6:20), were people of faith who protected him from being killed (Heb. 11:23). Like his parents, Moses became a man of faith (Heb. 11:24–28). What characteristics in Moses' faith are similar to those of his parents (Heb. 11:23–29)?

    b. In Heb. 11:13 and Heb. 11:27, the Bible mentions a distinguishing characteristic of all those who live by faith. What is it?

9. Faith is powerful enough to conquer cities (Jericho), transform lives (Rahab was a prostitute), subdue kingdoms, stop the mouths of lions (Daniel), and accomplish other supernatural events (Heb. 11:30–35). Men and women of God were tortured, ridiculed, mocked, stoned, imprisoned, scourged, and lived in caves and dens in the earth (Heb. 11:36–39).

    a. Why did they endure such ill-treatment (Heb. 11:35)?

    b. What did they receive for their willingness to live by faith (Heb. 11:39)?

10. Biblical faith is being sure of things we hope for (a present assurance of certain future event) and the willingness to trust God's promises and embrace them as our own.

    a. What evidences do you see in your life that you are living by faith?

    b. What evidences indicate that you are not living by faith?

13: A Race Called Faith

Read: Hebrews 12:1-29; other references as given.

Each day Christians enter a familiar race—a life-long marathon called living by faith. The race isn't run in competition with other believers, but alongside them. It isn't won by sitting comfortably in the stands (a.k.a. church pews), but by trusting God with the details of life and living each day empowered by the Holy Spirit for the glory of God.

In this lesson you'll learn how to win this race called faith. Now before you begin, ask God to reveal Himself through His Word and to give you the grace to accept the truths you will be learning.

1. In Hebrews 12:1–4, 12–13, the writer uses the analogy of an athletic race to help his readers grasp key truths about living by faith. There are three key aspects to running well: *preparation* (before the race), *focus* (before and during the race), and *perseverance* (throughout the race).

    a. The (cloud of) witnesses are the faithful saints who lived by faith and died. Their Christian testimonies serve as an inspiration to believers, encouraging them to live by faith and finish strong. What two things must a Christian do to properly prepare to live by faith (Heb. 12:1)?

    b. What two obstacles did Jesus have to overcome to be victorious on the cross, and upon what did He focus to accomplish His mission (Heb. 12:2)?

2. a. Believers are to **lay aside every weight** (Greek—*ogkos:* bulk, mass, weight; NIV—"everything that hinders") and the sin which so easily entangles us (Heb. 12:1). What do you think is the difference between a sin and a weight (Heb. 12:1)?

    b. What spiritual weights are you grudgingly holding onto that should be eliminated from your life?

        What should you do if they are keeping you from serving Christ more effectively?

3. When believers become weary and discouraged, they become ineffective servants for God. Upon what or whom should every Christian focus to prevent spiritual fatigue and discouragement (Heb. 12:3)?

4. The Jewish believers suffered persecution in the past (Heb. 10:32–34), but now were facing trouble of a different kind. God was disciplining the believers for their spiritual apathy (Heb. 12:5–11).

    a. Often Christians feel they're being persecuted when they are actually being chastened by God. How can a believer determine if his faith is being tested (like Job's faith) or if he is being chastised by God (like the Jewish believers, Gal. 6:7–8)?

    b. Name at least four benefits believers receive from God's chastening (Heb. 12:5–11).

5. In Hebrews 12:12–17, the writer returns to the race analogy. He confronts the Jewish believers' apathy (Heb. 12:12—**weak hands and feeble knees**) and exhorts them to make immediate changes to avoid serious spiritual injury (Heb. 12:13, **dislocation**, NIV—"disabled"). What five things must they (and all believers) do to strengthen their Christian lives (Heb. 12:14)?

6. a. Hebrews 12:15 says Christians must guard themselves against a **root of bitterness** (NIV—"bitter root"). Why do you think it is called a *root* of bitterness?

    b. What will happen if a believer doesn't truly forgive others (Matt. 18:34–35)?

7. Esau was a **profane** man (Greek—*bebelos:* profane, unhallowed, desecrated; NIV—"godless") (Heb. 12:16–17). Although he is mentioned in Hebrews 11:20, not one word of commendation is said about him. In Scripture, he's an example of someone who didn't value the things of God until it was too late.

    a.   The Jewish birthright was a special spiritual blessing given to the oldest son (in this case Esau). What did Esau say to indicate he regarded the things of God as having little value (Gen. 25:32)?

    b.   Many Christians believe God is obligated to restore everything they lost during a time of sinful behavior if they simply confess their sin. What important spiritual truth does Esau's sin and confession teach about forgiveness and spiritual restoration (Gen. 12:17)?

8.   Even though God is deadly serious about sin, Christians should live in hope and peace, not in fear and doubt. The writer presents a contrast between living near two mountains—Mount Sinai (Horeb), signifying the Old Covenant law (Heb. 12:18–21) and Mount Zion, signifying assurance of salvation and anticipation of heaven (Heb. 12:22–24).

    a.   Examine your life before God. Does your relationship with God indicate you are living (metaphorically) at Mount Sinai or at Mount Zion?

    b.   If a person mostly views God as a god of terror and punishment who must be constantly appeased, what does this indicate?

9.   Hebrews 12:25–29 offers the fifth and final *solemn warning.* The first *solemn warning* exhorts believers not to be <u>casual</u> about their salvation (Heb 2:1–4). The second *solemn warning* exhorts believers not to be <u>carnal</u> and forfeit God's promises (Heb. 3:7–4:13). The third *solemn warning* exhorts believers not to be <u>complacent</u> about their spiritual growth (Heb. 5:12–6:8). The fourth *solemn warning* exhorts believers not to be <u>callous</u> about intentional sin in their lives (Heb. 10:26–31).

    a.   Summarize the fifth solemn warning in one sentence. Try to show its distinctiveness from the other four warnings.

    b.   Within the immediate context, what do you think is the meaning of the phrase **For our God is a consuming fire** (Heb. 12:29)?

14: Changeless Christ, Timeless Truths

Read: Hebrews 13:1–25; other references as given.

The book of Hebrews concludes with several short exhortations (one to four verses) that provide practical instruction on virtuous Christian living. Believers are encouraged to live out their devotion to Christ through tangible expressions of godly behavior, bearing witness to a transformed life.

Each exhortation is presented in a spirit of tacit obedience. It is as if the writer is saying, *"If you have been truly transformed by Christ, it's only natural that you'll worship Christ and obey His commands in the details of life."* However, true devotion to Christ is more than mere external acts of compliance—it is submitting to Christ completely and transforming the routines of life into acts of private worship.

Before you begin, ask God to reveal Himself through His Word and to give you the grace to accept the truths you will be learning.

1. The writer encourages his readers to continue loving one another as brothers and sisters in Christ (Heb. 13:1). This encouragement indicates that a genuine love for one another already existed. List two additional people groups to whom the Jewish believers should express their love, and describe the manner in which their love was to be shown (Heb. 13:1–3).

2. The Bible says **marriage is honorable among all** (Heb. 13:4, NIV—"marriage should be honored by all"). God holds marriage in high regard, and severe warnings are given for those who violate His standards.

   a. Tragically, many people—including some believers—don't honor marriage. What do you think are some ways *Christians* dishonor marriage?

   b. What do you think every Christian should do to honor the institution of marriage? List at least five things.

3.   a.   What can a Christian expect if he doesn't honor God's standards of sexual purity (Heb. 13:4, Prov. 6:23–35, 7:6–27)?

   b.   If you are married, what specific commitments have you and your spouse made to God and each other to keep your marriage bed pure? If you are a Christian single, what specific commitments have you made to God and yourself to remain sexually pure?

4.   God commanded Adam and Eve to be fruitful and subdue the earth (Gen. 1:28). How can a Christian fulfill the commands to subdue the earth and **be content with such things as you have** (Heb. 13:5–6)?

5.   We are living in a day of diminished respect for God-ordained spiritual authority. What specific instruction did the writer give his readers about their conduct and attitude toward spiritual leaders, both past and present (Heb. 13:7, 17)?

6.   a.   **Jesus Christ is the same yesterday, today and forever** (Heb. 13:8). What does this mean (Malachi 3:6)?

   b.   Theologians use the term "immutability" to refer to Christ's changelessness of character. Christ's immutability is an indisputable doctrine of Scripture that has profound theological and practical consequences. Because Christ is immutable, God's Word can be trusted, God's promises are secure, and God's final judgments are inevitable. Now that you understand Christ's immutability, what do you think are some additional implications of this doctrine?

7.   In Hebrews 13:10, the writer returns to comparing the Old Covenant form of worship in the tabernacle and worship under the New Covenant, where **we have an altar from which those who serve the tabernacle have no right to eat** (Heb. 13:10). The Old Testament tabernacle was eventually replaced by King Solomon, who built a permanent temple in Jerusalem.

   a.   Churches often refer to the front of the church as the altar. Wedding guests refer to the same location in a church as a wedding altar. What do you think is this New Covenant altar, and where is it located (Heb. 13:10)?

   b.   Christians often say they are going to church when, in fact, they are the church. What this means is they're going to meet together as a church (1 Cor. 11:17). Christians also have a temple. Where or what is the temple for New Testament believers (1 Cor. 3:17-18, 6:19–20)?

   c.   Under the Old Covenant, worshippers offered various sacrifices. What sacrifices should Christians offer to God (Romans 12:1; Heb. 13:15–16)?

8.   What two final terms are used to describe Jesus Christ (Heb. 13:20)?

9.   Do you believe Jesus Christ offered one sacrifice on the cross to pay the complete penalty for your sin?

10.   The Old Testament Israelites had the gospel preached to them, **but the word which they heard did not profit them because it was not mixed with faith in those who heard it** (Heb. 4:2). What specific spiritual truths did you learn in this study of Hebrews that you are going to apply to your life?

Leader's Guide

Lesson 1 – *God's Ultimate Revelation*

1. a. The Bible is the inspired Word of God (2 Tim. 3:16). The individuals God used to write the Bible were supernaturally guided by the Holy Spirit so the words in the original manuscripts were inspired and inerrant.

   b. A brief word of exhortation. The Greek word for exhortation (*parakaleo*) can be translated to mean encourage or exhort. The letter's general tenor seems to favor exhortation because the writer uses direct language to challenge the readers to escape spiritual apathy and go on to spiritual maturity.

2. a. God spoke directly to Adam (Gen. 3:9–13). God spoke to Laban in a dream (Gen. 31:24). God revealed Himself to the prophets Ezekiel and Daniel in visions (Ezek. 1:1; Dan. 2:17–23). God revealed His will to His people through the prophets (Amos 3:7).

   b. God revealed Himself in the past (the Old Testament period) through the prophets at many times and in various ways, but He revealed Himself in these last days through Jesus Christ. The use of the Greek aorist tense to describe both the completion of God's revelation in the Old Testament era and His revelation through Jesus is significant. Jesus Christ is the fulfillment of the Old Testament prophets' prophecies and the completion of God's revelation to man. No new revelation from God should be expected by His people.

3. A believer should probably refrain from using a phrase like this to avoid giving the (erroneous) impression that God still provides new revelation to man. However, since many Christians use similar phrases to refer to the Holy Spirit's work in their lives (not new revelation from God), it would be wrong to constantly correct those who make innocent mistakes that can be easily interpreted in the believer's mind. Christians must realize that the work of sanctification is God's responsibility.

4. 1. He is God's son (v. 2). 2. He is God's the Father's final revelation in these last days (v. 2). 3. He is the heir of all things (v. 2). 4. He is the creator of the universe (v. 2). 5. He is the brightness of His glory (v. 3). 6. He is the express image of God, the Father's person (v. 3). 7. He upholds or sustains all things by the power of His word (v. 3). 8. He has paid man's complete sin debt (v. 3). 9. He has assumed a place of honor next to the Father (v. 3), and He is better than the angels (v. 4).

5. Jesus Christ is the very image or stamp of God the father. The normal Greek word for image is *eikon*, but in this phrase the Greek word *charakter* (from which we derive the English word character) is used and this is the only appearance of this word in the New Testament. The word refers to an engraved character or impression made by a die or seal. It is used with special reference to *distinguishing characteristics* that identify it with the original. Jesus Christ is the exact representation or express image of the father even though they are two separate entities.

6.   1.   (Heb. 1:5) Only Jesus is God's son.
     2.   (Heb. 1:6–7) Jesus receives worship, but the angels are only servants.
     3.   (Heb. 1:8–9) Only Jesus reigns supreme over an eternal kingdom.
     4.   (Heb. 1:10–12) Only Jesus is the eternal creator.
     5.   (Heb. 1:13–14) Jesus was invited to sit in the place of privilege at the father's right hand. Angels are servants who have been commissioned to serve believers.

7. The Greek word for firstborn (*prototokos*) can mean first in time or first in importance. The word refers to Christ's supreme status as first in importance in this world (as well as in the eternal state). It probably also refers to the privileged position of the firstborn son within the Jewish culture.

8. Angels serve as God's agents to gather the wicked for the final judgment (Matt. 13:36–42). Angels do not marry (Matt. 22:29–30). Angels rejoice over the salvation of individual souls (Luke 15:10). Angels are eternal (Luke 20:34–36). Angels are not omniscient. They have a desire to understand the things of God (1 Peter 1:10–12). They worship God in His very presence (Rev. 7:11–12).

9.   a.   Nothing is mentioned in the Bible about adult believers having guardian angels. Christians should focus their spiritual attention on Christ's presence, protection, and provision—not those who are merely servants of God.
     b.   An unbiblical focus on angels can lead to worship of angels (Col. 2:18) and violating God's prohibition to not place any other gods before Him (Exod. 20:3).

Lesson 2 – *Captain of Our Salvation*

1. If believers neglect their salvation they will drift away from God (Heb. 2:1). They will experience God's chastening (Heb. 2:2–3).

2.   a.   If believers neglect (not reject) their salvation they will experience God's discipline in their lives. The passage does not specify what type of chastening they will receive. The writer uses the Old Testament account of the Israelites' exodus from Egypt as an example of God's willingness to punish His people. He said *every* transgression and act of disobedience received a just (or appropriate) reward. Many Christians believe the close relationship between disobedience and punishment was limited to the Old Testament era, but the principle of sowing (to his flesh) and reaping the consequences of our error is applied here to New Testament believers and in Galatians 6:8–9.
     b.   Answers will vary, but could include the following: sporadic church involvement, inconsistent personal Bible reading, little prayer, limited fellowship with other believers, a cavalier attitude toward sinful attitudes and actions in his life and others, an inordinate focus on the love of God as a mask for tolerating sin.
     c.   Answers will vary.

3. Answers will vary.

4. God allowed those who originally received the words of Christ to perform signs and wonders. God also equipped them to do miracles and the Holy Spirit gave them spiritual gifts to authenticate the message they had received from Christ. These supernatural gifts were given to them according to God's will rather than a reward for spirituality.

5. God's revelation is a gift from God through the ministry of the Holy Spirit. Nowhere in the Bible do the Scriptures attribute the ultimate source of Scripture to man's ability. Christians should be careful to maintain a biblical perspective on the doctrine of inspiration.

6. In the larger context, the writer is arguing for Christ's superiority over angels (Heb. 1:5–2:9). The writer quotes from an Old Testament passage to prove his point, not to introduce a separate thought that has little relevance to the original topic. Secondly, the quotation is used help explain Christ's incarnation (when he became a man) to demonstrate that man's present weakness and ineptitude is only temporary. Man will again be crowned with glory and we see the first fruits of this transformation in the risen Christ.

7. Christ has ultimate authority over heaven and earth at the present time (Matt. 28:18). God has given the forces of evil (in this case, a Roman governor Pilate) limited authority to accomplish their wicked plans within the decretive will of God (John 19:10–11). Christ has given Satan some degree of authority over all the nations of this world (Matt. 3:8–9). God's people should pray for the establishment of God's rule on earth and for the kingdom of God to be realized (Matt. 6:8–13). God's rule and kingdom will come to earth and become and everlasting kingdom at the end of the tribulation period (Rev. 11:15). When Christ's kingdom is established on earth, Satan (the accuser of our brethren) will be cast down (Rev. 12:10).

8. a. Christ became a man (like His brethren) and was tempted in every way we are, but He never sinned. He is a merciful and faithful High Priest. He is merciful in the sense that He understands our weakness. He was faithful to fulfill His role as High Priest by providing an acceptable sacrifice to God for the forgiveness of sins. The sacrifice offered was His own body.
   b. Even though Christ's sacrifice for sins was a once-for-all offering, He continues to serve as the believer's High Priest. He makes intercession for believers every time they sin. Christians should remember that the complete payment of sin was paid, but Christ continues to make intercession on our behalf every time we sin.

Lesson 3 – *Doubt in the Desert*

1. In Hebrews 3:1, the writer was referring to the Jewish believers' *position* in Christ. These Jewish believers (and all Christians) are holy brethren (collective plural for brothers and sisters) in their legal standing before God. They have been set apart for God's glory at the time of salvation. All believers are holy brethren and have been made partakers of a holy calling—the high calling of Christ. In Hebrews 5:11 and 6:12, the writer refers to the Jewish believers' *practice* or spiritual conduct. Like many Christians of every generation, their conduct didn't live up to their calling in Christ.

2. The command means to stay continually focused on Christ. The Greek word means to "put the mind down on a thing" and expresses attention, continuous observation, and regard. To consider Jesus means the believer examines his thoughts, attitudes, and actions in light of God's Word and diligently brings them into captivity and conformity to Christ. The familiar phrase "What would Jesus do?" partially captures the heart of an individual who wants to fulfill this command.

3. God's Word often makes summary judgments about individuals' lives from the perspective of their overall devotion to Him. The Bible says Moses was faithful in His (God's) house, which is likely a reference to the tabernacle. The book of Second Chronicles mentions several kings who "did right in the sight of the Lord" but then the text mentions some of the failures. God doesn't ignore sin in our lives, but He seems to acknowledge the general tenor of a man's life without focusing on a single failure—an important spiritual lesson to remember.

4. a. Both were faithful to fulfill the ministries God the Father assigned them to do (Heb. 3:2).
    b. 1. Jesus is worthy of more glory than Moses (Heb. 3:2). 2. Moses was a faithful servant over the house of God, but Jesus was the builder of the house of God (Heb. 3:3–4). Moses was a servant and didn't own the house, but Jesus is the owner of all things (Heb. 3:5–6).

5. a. These two phrases refer to the period of time between the Jews' exodus from Egypt and the death of Moses forty years later.
    b. The Israelites did not experience God's rest during those forty years. God was angry with that generation of Israelites for forty years.

6. a. Eleven days. b. Answers will vary. c. Answers will vary.

7. Inheritance, protection from their enemies.

8. a. Sin is a deceiver because it never delivers what it promises. Sin is also a distraction because it takes us away from God. When we sin, our hearts become hardened against God, and our minds become insensitive to the promises of God's blessing and His promise of chastisement. Sin deceives us into thinking

that God's ways are not best, His commands are not good, and His judgments are not certain.

b.   1. Believers must assume the personal responsibility of not allowing unbelief to enter our lives (Heb.3:12). 2. Believers are commanded to encourage one another in the things of the Lord daily (Heb. 3:13).

9.   Both verses are teaching the same important spiritual truth. The real test of a believer's faith is determined by whether he remains faithful to the Lord until the end of his life. We are part of God's house (Heb. 3:6) and become partakers of Christ *if* we demonstrate the type of faith that maintains confidence in Christ and rejoices in the promises He has given us in His Word. A faith that doesn't maintain this confidence and hope falls short of salvation, regardless of what the individual professes to believe.

Lesson 4 – *Promise of God's Rest*

1.   a.   1.   Both *rests* were guaranteed—they are based upon God's offer/promise and He doesn't lie.

   2.   The only contingency for entering the rest is the Christian's faith/belief (Heb. 3:19, 4:11).

   3.   In both situations, there is a real possibility of missing the rest God promised (Heb. 3:18, 4:11).

   b.   The Israelites didn't apply God's Word to their lives, even though they heard the truth.

   c.   Faith or belief.

2.   Romans 15:4—Christians gain encouragement and hope as they see God working out His will in the lives of His people. When believers see that God is the "watcher of men" and rewards or punishes man accordingly, they are encouraged to trust and obey Him more. This builds spiritual perseverance and faith in God's people.
1 Cor. 10:1–11—Christians can learn from the failures of many Old Testament people whose lives serve as examples of what not to do. Christians can learn what punishment they should expect from God if they repeat the same sins (1 Cor. 10:6–11).

3.   This *rest* does not refer to salvation because salvation is a free gift from God, not something we work diligently to gain (Heb. 4:11). This rest is supernatural peace all God's people (lest <u>anyone</u> come short of it) can experience on a daily basis as a result of fully trusting God's Word, His will, and His ways. The rest comes progressively into a believer's life as he learns to walk with God and trust Him. God's rest is such a great spiritual privilege that all believers should fear lest any miss it (Heb. 4:1) and every believer should be diligent to enter it (Heb. 4:11).

4.   Resting in the Lord is a spiritual virtue, but slothfulness is a sin. Resting in the Lord is trusting God, but laziness is not trusting/disobeying the Lord who commanded His

people to work. Resting in the Lord is active faith, but slothfulness is a sin against God.

5. 1. Christians must believe God has given them a promise (Heb. 4:1, 9). 2. Christians must believe it's God's will for every believer, including them, to experience His rest (Heb. 4:1). 3. Christians must understand that we enter God's rest through faith (Heb. 4:3). 4. Christians must realize disobedience prevents them from entering into God's rest (Heb. 4:6). 5. Christians must be diligent to live by faith if they expect to enter God's rest (Heb. 4:11).

6. Only God's Word possesses the power to expose the Christians' sinful motives and actions, which often lead to disobedience and keep him from experiencing rest.

7. a. God's Word is His living revelation to man. Because men of God spoke *as they were* moved by the Holy Spirit (2 Peter 1:21), the Bible is living. By "living," we don't mean it is constantly changing; we mean it possesses a supernatural power to change lives.

   b. God's Word is also powerful or energetic, active, and productive. The Greek word *energes* is often used for divine activity which produces effective results. It takes something powerful and productive to convict the believer when he is in error, confirm him when his motives are centered in God's will, and transform his life. Only God's Word possesses this power.

   c. God's Word functions as a spiritual scalpel to separate thoughts and attitudes that are born of the Spirit of God from those born in the heart of man. The inner life of a Christian is often a mixture of pure and impure motives and fleshly and spiritual thoughts. God's Word is able to search out the most intimate thoughts and intents of man's innermost being. Because only God's Word possesses this supernatural power, His Word should be the central focus of all Christian preaching and teaching.

8. They must recognize that God's omniscience (His ability to see and know everything immediately) extends to their innermost thoughts and be completely transparent before Him, knowing they will give account to Him in the final judgment. When a believer understands this truth, he will be more willing to confess his secret sins and gain God's rest.

9. Jesus can sympathize with our sinful nature because He was tempted in every way known to man, yet he never sinned (Heb. 4:15). He has given us a bold invitation to approach Him anytime we need mercy and grace (Heb. 4:16).

Lesson 5 – *Apathy Alert*

1.   a.   1. They were men (Heb. 5:1). 2. They were appointed rather than having volunteered for the position   (Heb. 5:1). 3. They represented men (for men) before God (Heb. 5:1). 4. Their primary responsibility was to offer gifts and sacrifices for sins (Heb. 5:1).
      b.   They were sinful and offered sacrifices for themselves and the people they served (Heb. 5:2–3).

2.   a.   The sage or wise man, and the prophet.
      b.   Apostle, prophet, evangelist, pastor-teacher.

3.   A priest represents man before God, and an elder/pastor represents God before men. The priest presents man's gifts to God, and the elder/pastor offers God's gifts (His Word, salvation) to man.

4.   a.   Consecration of the Jewish firstborn served as a perpetual reminder to future generations that the Lord delivered the Israelites out of Egypt with a mighty hand. It also reminded the Jews that God judged their enemies. He punished Pharaoh for his stubbornness by killing the Egyptian firstborn.
      b.   While the text doesn't specifically say why the Lord replaced the firstborn with the Levites, His reason may have been one of practicality. Aaron and his son Eleazar were Levites. God commissioned Eleazar to oversee the Levites and the number of the Levites was 22,000. The number of all the firstborn one month old and older was 22, 273 (Num. 3:39, 43).
      c.   The Levites were to serve Aaron (Num. 3:6), serve the whole Israelite congregation and attend to the things of the tabernacle (Num. 3:7–8). They were responsible for setting up, dissembling, and moving the tabernacle every time the Lord directed the people to move (Num. 3:8).

5.   a.   Jesus serves as the High Priest, and individual believers serve as the priests.
      b.   1.   There is only one mediator between God and man and His name is Jesus Christ. No other name qualifies, because only Jesus is the perfect and acceptable sacrifice (1 Tim. 2:5–6).
          2.   Jesus is alive and serves as our High Priest to make intercession for believers (Heb. 7:25).
          3.   Christians don't need a priest because they already have one (Heb. 8:1).

6.   In Hebrews 5:5–6, the writer quotes two Old Testament passages, Psalms 2:7 and 110:4, to prove it was God Himself who appointed and commissioned Jesus as High Priest according to a different priestly order—the order of Melchizedek.

7.   1.   Jesus was heard because of His godly fear (Heb. 5:7).
      2.   Jesus was perfected, meaning that he was glorified when he was resurrected (Heb. 5:9).

3.   He became the author of eternal salvation to all who obey Him (Heb. 5:9, only those who are redeemed can really obey God).

8.   Since every Jewish priest under the Old Covenant had to come from the tribe of Levi, the writer had to explain that Jesus was of a different priestly order (the order of Melchizedek). By quoting two key passages from the Old Testament Psalms, the writer demonstrates the historicity and veracity of Jesus' claim to be a priest—a priest of a different priestly order, with solid biblical authority.

9.   a.   God's expected time for all Christians to be spiritually mature.
     b.   Milk is the food of babies and is used to refer to the simple teachings and doctrines of the Bible. Solid food is for more the more mature and refers to the more advanced doctrines in God's Word.
     c.   1. They had stunted spiritual development (Heb. 5:12–13). 2. They couldn't communicate God's Word to others (Heb. 5:12). 3. They regressed in their spiritual lives to the point that they need to be taught again the basic doctrines of the Bible (Heb. 5:12). 4. They had become unskilled in the Word (Heb. 5:13). 5. Their lack of spiritual development produced a lack of discernment (Heb. 5:14).
     d.   Answers will vary.

Lesson 6 – *It's Time to Grow Up*

1.   1.   The Jewish believers (and all Christians) were encouraged to move beyond the basic teachings in God's Word.
     2.   They were to grow to spiritual maturity. The Greek word (*telos*) can be translated complete or perfect. When it is used of a believer's relationship to God, it indicates His expectation for all Christians to reach spiritual mature in Christ.

2.   a.   The Greek phrase (*teo arches tou Christou logon*) is literally translated "the word of the beginning of Christ." It means the beginning teachings about Christ or Christ's initial teachings. Most translations translate the phrase (which can be translated either way) as the former.
     b.   They are the deeds done by an individual that lead to death. In the immediate context, the word "works" seems to imply they are religious in nature—perhaps deeds done with the hope of bringing life, but only producing death.
     c.   Answer will vary.

3.   a.   Spirit Baptism, the work of the Holy Spirit, occurs the time of conversion (salvation) to Christ (1 Cor. 12:13; Titus 3:5). Spirit Baptism applies the sacrifice of Christ's death on the cross to the sin debt of the individual, effectively accomplishes the work of regeneration, and places an individual into the body of Christ. Water Baptism (often called Believer's Baptism) occurs after conversion and is an initial step of obedience and a powerful testimony for Christ.
     b.   Believer's Baptism is an outward expression of an individual Christian's inward conversion and Spirit Baptism. It a public witness that expresses the prior work of the Holy Spirit at the time of conversion to Christ.

4.   a.   1.   They were once enlightened.

           2.   They had tasted the heavenly gift.

           3.   They had become partakers of the Holy Spirit.

           4.   They had tasted of the good Word of God.

           5.   They had tasted the power of the age to come.

     b.   Believers.

           1.   The immediate context is an exhortation and warning to believers. It would seem rather hollow to warn believers with an example that only directly applies to non-believers.

           2.   The Greek word tasted (*geuomai*) doesn't mean sample as some interpreters suggest. The same Greek word, used of Christ's death on the cross—"He tasted death for everyone" (Heb. 2:9)—describes His full embrace of the cross.

           3.   Only believers become partakers of the Holy Spirit.

     c.   1.   Those who fall away enter into such a state of advance spiritual deception that other believers can't convince them of their error.

           2.   They crucify "Christ all over again" by turning their back on His sacrifice to redeem them and save them for a life of sin. This doesn't mean they lose their salvation. It means their lives are so sinful that it is as if Christ had to go to the cross all over again.

           3.   They bring shame on Christ's name because they accepted Christ and then turned away from His mercy and grace. This behavior always brings shame to Christ's name.

5.   a.   The latter. The passage is saying that it is impossible for a committed Christian to renew a believer who has entered a state of advanced spiritual deception (those who have fallen away). Like the prodigal son, only God can reach the individual. Since believers can't be sure when this happens, they should attempt to reach believers who have fallen away from the Lord until the Holy Spirit directs them otherwise (1 Cor. 5:4–5).

     b.   The committed believers who are powerless to reach those who have fallen away from the Lord.

     c.   If a believer is complacent about his relationship with Christ, he will become spiritually insensitive to God (Heb. 5:12) and begins to regress in his spiritual life. If he continues in this path, he will develop a lack of discernment (Heb. 5:14) and even begin to question basic Bible doctrine (Heb. 6:1–2). If he thinks he can turn God on and off at any time, he is dreadfully wrong, because spiritual growth (sanctification) is God's work (Heb. 6:3). If the believer continues toward spiritual self-deception, he will eventually get to the place in his spiritual life where no committed Christian can convince him he is wrong. God will eventually chasten the believer even to the point of removing everything for which he has worked (Heb. 6:7–8).

6. Everything the ground has yielded is burned completely.

7. a. The fruit of the ground is burned. The burning removes the weeds so the ground can be productive in the future.
    b. The ground is free to produce good crops.
8. a. Answers will vary.
    b. 1. God testified that His counsel doesn't change (the immutability/changelessness of His counsel), and He confirmed this promise with His oath (Heb. 6:17).
        2. It's impossible for God to lie (Heb. 6:18).
    c. Believers should lay hold (NIV—"take hold") of God's promises, personalizing and possessing them so they become a living reality and refuge (Heb. 6:18). The believer shouldn't consider God's promises as distant wishes that may someday be realized. He should allow God's promises to anchor his soul during the storms of life (Heb. 6:19). The believer should regard God's promises, including those that assure the believer of full and complete acceptance into the Presence of God through the blood of Christ, as firm secure, and guaranteed.

Lesson 7 – *Mysterious Melchizedek*

1. a. Melchizedek was the king of Salem and priest of the God Most High (Gen. 14:18). He was a contemporary of the patriarch Abraham and received tithe from him. The phrase *Most High God* means that he worshipped and served the one true God. The same phrase is used of Abram (Abraham) and we know Abraham worshipped the true God (Gen. 14:19). Melchizedek was the head of a priestly order that was distinct from the Levitical Priesthood (Psalm 110:4). His name (perhaps a title rather than a proper name) meant "king of righteousness" and "king of peace" (Heb. 7:2). Nothing is known about his earthly heritage (Heb. 7:3).
    b. Priest and king.

2. a. He has a specific name or title (Heb. 7:1). Abraham gave him a tithe of the spoils of war and Melchizedek received them (Heb. 7:2). He is identified him as a man (Heb. 7:4). He has a genealogy—it is just not given (Heb. 7:6).
    b. It doesn't mean that Melchizedek was a biological anomaly or angel in human disguise, since the immediate context clearly identifies him as a mortal. It simply means that nothing is recorded in Scripture about this individual and it is if he was without earthly heritage. Moreover, since there is no record of his birth or death it is as if he was eternal. The writer's point is to show the similarities between Melchizedek and Christ, whose birth and death were also shrouded in mystery and He is an eternal priest and a king.

3. Answers will vary.

4. a. Every Jew knows Abraham was great man of God. If Abraham was a great Jew

and he gave (paid) a tithe to Melchizedek, this proves Abraham must have believed that he (Melchizedek) was a legitimate priest.

b. Since Levi was the great-grandson of Abraham, he was in the loins (NIV—body) of Abraham when the original tithe was paid to Melchizedek. And even though the Levites received tithes from the Jews, they also paid them figuratively when Abraham paid tithe and Levi was still in him (Heb. 7:9–10)

5. "Before Abraham was, I am."

6. If perfection came through the Old Testament law and the Levitical priesthood, there wouldn't have been the need for a second order of priests. The very existence of a second order of priest (the Melchizedekian priesthood) proves that something was imperfect with the Levitical priesthood.

7. There must be a change in the law.

8. 1. Both functioned in the dual role as priest and king (Heb. 7:2; Mark 15:26). 2. Both names are synonymous with righteousness and peace. 3. Both are from the same priestly line.

9.

	Levitical Priesthood	Christ's Priesthood
a. Priestly tribe	_____Levi_____ (Heb. 7:11)	_____Judah_____ (Heb. 7:14)
b. Ability to redeem	made nothing perfect (Heb. 7:19)	able to save (Heb. 7:25)
c. Number of Priests	_____many_____ (Heb. 7:23)	only one—Jesus (Heb. 7:24)
d. Priest's character	_sinful_ (Heb. 7:27-28)	holy, harmless, undefiled (Heb. 7:26)
e. Number of offerings	_____daily_____ (Heb. 7:27)	once for all_____ (Heb. 7:27)

Lesson 8 – A New and Living Way to God

1. a. Christians have a high priest who is alive and seated at the right hand of God in heaven.
   b. The Jewish Christians to whom the book of Hebrews was written and all those who are truly saved through faith in Jesus Christ.

2. a. Both forms of worship have high priests (Heb. 8:1, 3). Both forms of worship have

sanctuaries and tabernacles. In both systems the high priest offers gifts and sacrifices to God (Heb. 8:3).

   b.   Jesus is seated, but the Jewish high priest is always standing (Heb. 8:1, 10:11). The seated position signifies Jesus' finished work, and the high priest's standing signifies his unfinished work. Jesus serves in the true tabernacle while the Jewish high priest served in a temporary earthly tabernacle (Heb. 8:1–2). The Lord erected the true tabernacle in heaven once, but man had to repeatedly erect the earthly tabernacle in the wilderness (Heb. 8:1–2).

3.   The Old Testament tabernacle and the objects served as a copy (Greek— *hypodeigmati*) and shadow (*skia*) of the heavenly one in which Jesus ministers. The two words, copy and shadow, are similar, but not exact synonyms. The word *copy* signifies substance and the word *shadow* signifies a reflection. Just as the high priest was a copy and a shadow or reflection of a future high priest (Jesus) who would serve as an eternal High Priest, the earthly tabernacle reflected the eternal sanctuary and true tabernacle in heaven. There are at least four Old Testament references that emphasize that Moses was to construct the earthly tabernacle according to God's exact specifications (Exod. 25:40, 26:30. 27:8; Num. 8:4).

4.   1. Jesus defeated the devil, and the power of death has been broken for those who are redeemed (Heb. 2:14–15). 2. God offers all Christians the promise of rest (God's perfect peace in the midst of life's storms) that can be entered by faith (Heb. 4:9). 3. God promised all believers direct access to God because of Jesus' sacrifice and who also serves as our High Priest (Heb. 6:19–20). 4. God is able to save "to the uttermost" those who come to Him through Christ (Heb. 7:25).

5.   a.   1. The first covenant (Heb. 8:7). 2. The ministry of death (2 Cor. 3:7). 3. The ministry of condemnation (2 Cor. 3:9).

   b.   The Old Covenant brought the knowledge of sin and death (Rom. 7:7–8). It was designed to expose sin and was a moral standard that no man could attain (Rom. 7:9–10).

6.   The Old Testament Law reflects the moral standard of God (Gal. 3:19). The Law confronts man with his sin and functions as a tutor or schoolmaster to show him his need for a savior (Gal. 3:25). Once the Law delivers a man to Christ by showing him his sin, it has fulfilled its function. Grace, not law, serves as a guiding principle in his life (Gal. 3:25).

7.   a.   Many Bible scholars believe the New Covenant was initiated at the time of Christ's crucifixion, when the curtain separating the Holy Place from the Holy of Holies was torn in two (Matt. 27:51). Jesus celebrated the coming of the New Covenant the night before with the apostles (Matt. 26:26–30). Other conservative scholars believe the New Covenant will not begin until the Millennium Kingdom.

   b.   The Old Covenant was made obsolete with coming of the New Covenant. The Old Covenant is growing old (NIV—"aging") in the sense that its time has passed and its usefulness in nearly finished. The old covenant vanishing away (NIV—

"will soon disappear") means that it has nearly ended. Within less than ten years after the writing of Hebrews, the Jerusalem temple (built by Herod), a permanent replica of the temporary tabernacle, was destroyed by the Romans in 70 AD.

Lesson 9 – *The New Covenant*

1. a. The lampstand, the table, and the showbread (Heb. 9:2).
    b. The golden censor, the arc of the covenant. Inside the arc of the covenant was a golden pot with manna in it (Exod. 16:9–36), Aaron's rod that budded (cf. Num. 17:1–13), and the tablets of stone Moses received from God (Heb. 9:4).

2. 1. The highly restricted nature of the Holiest of All indicated a direct approach to God wasn't available through the Old Testament form of worship (Heb. 9:8).
    2. The repeat offerings of the sacrifices taught that the people's sin was never completely atoned (Heb. 9:9). The regular offerings were never able to give the priests or the people complete assurance (cannot make him who performs the service perfect in regard to conscience). The Old Testament sacrificial system addressed the problem of individual sins, but never dealt with the concept of sin as a whole.

3. a. The high priest confessed all the Israelite's national iniquities and transgressions (Lev. 16:21).
    b. It was a personal and symbolic identification with the sin bearer (the scapegoat) and transfer of Israel's sins to the scapegoat. In the same way, man must identify personally with Christ as his scapegoat at the time of salvation if he wants Him to be his sin-bearer.

4. 1. Jesus was bound and led by the Roman soldiers in the same way the scapegoat would have been bound and led away by the high priest (John 1:6–7).
    2. Jesus was led outside the place of worship (Jerusalem) to bear the sins of the world and the scapegoat was led outside the tabernacle and released into the wilderness (John 16:6–7).
    3. Jesus and the scapegoat were sin-bearers (2 Peter 2:24).

5. a. Believers are to pursue Christ and love Him with all the heart, soul, mind, and strength. They are to leave behind everything that hinders their spiritual journey (Heb. 12:1–2) and keep their eyes on Christ. In the immediate context, these Jewish readers were being commanded to leave the camp of Judaism (originally Israel camped in the wilderness).
    b. Christians must believe the cross of Jesus Christ always brings reproach. Believers shouldn't shrink back from bearing the reproach that comes from identifying fully with Jesus. Believers shouldn't attempt to make the cross less offensive to the world through compromise. Christians must realize the world will always embrace religion as long as we don't speak about the cross of Jesus Christ and proclaim the absolute need for all men to be saved. Believers must go

outside the camp, bearing His reproach—there is no other way to see a lost world escape a Christ-less eternity.

    c.   Answers will vary.

6.   1.   Conscience—Under the Old Covenant, the worshipper's conscience wasn't fully cleansed with regard to sin (Heb. 9:9). Under the New Covenant, the believer's conscience is cleansed and he is freed from all guilt pertaining to sins, past, present, and future (Heb. 9:14).

      2.   Tabernacle—Jesus offers a greater and more perfect tabernacle than the one offered in Judaism (Heb. 9:11).

      3.   Blood—Under the Old Covenant, the repeat offerings of goats and calves' blood couldn't obtain eternal redemption. Under the New Covenant, Christ's blood obtained eternal redemption for all who trust Him by faith (Heb. 9:12).

      4.   Inheritance—Under the Old Covenant, worshippers received no inheritance, but under the New Covenant, those who are called receive the promise of the eternal inheritance (Heb. 9:15).

7.   Good conscience (Acts 23:1). Weak conscience (1 Cor. 8:7). Pure conscience (1 Tim. 3:9). Seared conscience (1 Tim. 4:2). Defiled conscience (Titus 1:15). Cleansed conscience (Heb. 9:14). Evil conscience (Heb. 10:22).

8.   a.   1.   To initiate the provisions of the New Covenant (Heb. 9:16–17).

         2.   To become that acceptable sacrifice to God the Father so He (Jesus) could appear in the presence of God for us (Heb. 9:24, as High Priest).

         3.   To offer Himself as the complete sacrifice for sin (Heb. 9:26).

      b.   Not that He should offer often (Heb. 9:25). Once (Heb. 9:26). Offered once (Heb. 9:27).

      c.   All men will be judged (by God).

Lesson 10 – *One Sacrifice for All Time*

1.   As a shadow of the good things to come, but not the very or exact image (Greek—*eikon*) of the things it represents.

2.   a.   1.   The Law showed man he had to made atonement for his sins.

         2.   The Law showed man he couldn't make atonement for his own sins. He needed a sacrifice.

         3.   The Law showed man that his sin kept him from having direct access to God.

         4.   The Law showed man he was a sinner.

      b.   New covenant provisions such as eternal redemption, a cleansed conscience, a merciful, faithful and perfect High Priest, etc.

      c.   The Law didn't accurately reflect the complete forgiveness of sins that is available through Jesus Christ. The Law did accurately reflect the cleansing of the conscience that could only come through Christ's sacrifice. The Law didn't accurately reflect the assurance of redemption that an individual could experience.

3. a. The Old Testament sacrifices couldn't assure the worshipper that his sins were forgiven before God. The Jews lived in a theocracy, with God as their ruler. The sacrificial system, including the confession of sin and the sacrifices, was designed to abrogate individual sins (not the individual's sin) and restore him to the Israelite community. The Day of Atonement was initiated to provide atonement for the Israelites' sins before God during the past year. Since the Day of Atonement was an annual event, the worshippers never had the complete confidence or assurance that future sins would be forgiven. In this sense, it is impossible for the blood of bulls and goats to take away sin before God eternally.

    b. 1. Under the Old Covenant, sacrifices could not perfect the worshipper (Heb. 10:1), but Christ's sacrifice sanctified believers forever (Heb. 10:10).
       2. Under the Old Covenant, there were continual sacrifices (Heb. 10:1), but Jesus offered only one sacrifice (Heb. 10:10).
       3. Under the Old Covenant God required sacrifices (Heb. 10:1), but under the New Covenant Jesus becomes the sacrifice (Heb. 10:10).
       4. The Old Covenant was taken away (Heb. 10:9) and the New Covenant was established (Heb. 10:9). Other answer could apply.

4. Jesus offered one sacrifice for sins forever (Heb. 10:12). By one offering He has perfected forever (Heb. 10:14). Their sins and lawless deeds I will remember no more (Heb. 10:17). There is no longer an offering for sin (Heb. 10:18).

5. Christ is seated at the right hand of God (Heb. 10:12). His seated position signifies that an offering for sin is no longer needed (Heb. 10:18).

6. a. Believers have boldness to enter the Holiest Place by the blood of Jesus.
    b. The veil in the temple was torn in two from top to bottom (Mark 15:38).

7. 1. Believers are to draw near to God in full assurance of faith (Heb. 10:22).
    2. Believers are to hold fast the profession of faith without wavering (Heb. 10:23).
    3. Believers should encourage one another to love and good works (Heb. 10:24).

8. Believers are commanded to encourage other Christians.

9. a. There is no longer a sacrifice for sins and they can expect God's fiery indignation and judgment.
    b. If a believer intentionally turns away from God and the Holy Spirit's conviction, then he is rejecting the grace of God and quenching the Holy Spirit in his life. He is rejecting the only One who can bring him back to the light and there is no sacrifice he can bring to God for his sin other than a repentant heart.
    c. God will repay them for their willful or intentional sin. They can expect God's stern judgment for their rebellion against Him.

10. The Jewish believers were not to give up the faith in God (Heb. 10:35) and they were to exercise spiritual endurance in the midst of the struggles because God would ultimately reward them (Heb. 10:36).

Lesson 11 – *The Definition of Faith*

1. a. Answers will vary.
   b. General faith believes in the existence of God and moral goodness of Jesus Christ. A person with general faith may even believe in God's inherent virtue, as well as His ability to answer prayer and perform miracles. But general faith isn't sufficient to save an individual from eternal damnation. Saving faith, on the other hand, accepts what God's Word teaches about man's sinful condition, and gives an individual the faith to trust Jesus alone for eternal life.

2. a. 1. Religious people who apparently performed good works in Jesus' name, but were rejected by Christ at the final judgment (in that day, Matt. 7:21–23). 2. Orthodox Jews who believed in the one true God but rejected Christ (John 8:37–44). 3. The devil and his demons (James 2:19).
   b. Paul encouraged the Corinthians to examine themselves (really their faith) to determine if their faith was a genuine, saving faith. Paul's firsthand knowledge of the Corinthian church (factions, immorality, lawsuits, pride) caused him to wonder whether many of the professing Christians within the church were really born again.
   c. Answers will vary.

3. a. Biblical faith is the present assurance that God is real, His Word is true, and His promises will be fulfilled. Biblical faith is not mystically declaring some impressions to be the "word of the Lord," nor is it claiming some conditional promise from God's Word as His absolute will for all believers. Biblical faith is trusting God and obeying His Word during the blessings and trials of life.
   b. The input of God's Word into his life (Rom. 10:17) and obedience to the things he hears (Heb. 4:2).

4. a. Faith and reason. Biblical faith receives God's revelation to man and then applies to various life circumstances according to the wisdom of God. When Paul received a vision from God, he shared what had been revealed to him with others and together they concluded that the Lord had called them to go into Europe (Acts 16:10). The Bible says by faith we understand (Heb. 11:3).
   b. The natural (unregenerate) man doesn't possess the capacity to comprehend the things of God (1 Cor. 2:14) because Satan (the god of this world) has blinded his mind to the truth (2 Cor. 4:4). Only believers have the capacity to comprehend the things of God. They can start with faith and understand the origin of the worlds and many other spiritual concepts that cannot be understood by the unregenerate. Christians shouldn't be afraid of arguing from faith to reason. In the scientific world, researchers start with the unproven thesis and test their

assertions in an attempt to prove their original belief. It takes a step of faith (unproven beliefs or assumptions) to begin the discovery process.

5.   a.   By faith, Abel worshipped in a manner that was acceptable to God.
     b.   By faith, Enoch lived a God-honoring life and God took him to heaven before he died.
     c.   By faith, Noah, acting out of fear of God, saved his family by preparing an ark for his family and himself.
     d.   By faith, Abraham obeyed and trusted God to fulfill His promise and give him an inheritance. Abraham was so convinced that God would keep His word that he left his family, lived in tents in a foreign land, and passed down the promise the next generation.
     e.   By faith, Sarah received the strength to conceive because she trusted God to fulfill His promise to give her and Abraham a child. Sarah's story is interesting because she originally doubted God's promise when the angelic messengers informed her that a son would be born to Abraham and her. She laughed within herself (Gen. 18:9–15) and their son Isaac's name means "laughter."

6.   a.   Without faith it's impossible to please God.
     b.   Christ asked a rhetorical question about whether he will find faith on the earth when He returns.

Lesson 12 – *Triumph of Faith*

1.   a.   They were strangers and pilgrims (NIV—"aliens and strangers") on the earth.
     b.   1.   They saw God's promises, meaning they understood them and believed the promises applied to them.
         2.   They were assured (NIV—"welcomed") in their own minds that God's promises were true.
         3.   They embraced God's promises, meaning they personally appropriated them to their lives.

2.   Believers who live by faith declare plainly that they are looking for another home—heaven.

3.   a.   The believer who lives by faith focuses his heart and mind on the eternal—a heavenly country. Therefore their attention and desire is not for this world and they are not drawn back into the passions and priorities of a fallen world. An ability to live above the earthly temptations of this world is a distinguishing characteristic of all those who live by faith. As a result, God is not ashamed to be called their God and He is preparing an eternal home for them.
     b.   Answers will vary.

4.   Overcoming the world means to live victoriously over a world system that relentlessly attacks the hearts and minds of man. Satan is the god of this world (2 Cor. 4:4) and he promotes a value system that is diametrically opposed to God. This value system

panders to the carnal desires of fallen man and seeks to entrap him in a maze of pleasure-first schemes that ultimately are designed to destroy him. Faith is the key to overcoming the lure of satanic enticement. The believer who lives by faith looks for a better resurrection and a better country—one that is based upon the virtue and fidelity of the one true God.

5.   a.   God promised Abram (Abraham) a natural-born child would be born to him. The child of promise (Isaac) would become Abraham's heir and his descendents would be as numerous as the stars (Gen. 15:4–5).
      b.   After Isaac was born, God tested Abraham by commanding him to offer Isaac as a burnt offering on one of the mountains He would show him. The spot where God led Abraham is Temple Mount in Jerusalem, where the Islamic Dome of the Rock now sits.
      c.   To trust God's original promise and sacrifice Isaac or to distrust God's original promise and spare his son. Like most of the steps of faith God's people face, the choices are simple. It is the obedience/stepping out in faith that is hard.
      d.   1.   Abraham rose early the next day. He didn't equivocate (Gen. 22:3).
            2.   Abraham brought everything he needed to follow through. He brought wood (Gen. 22:3), fire and a knife (Gen. 22:6), and he didn't turn back. He bound Isaac and raised the knife to kill his son. He didn't play games with God.
            3.   Abraham had a plan to leave the servants at a particular place and he had an answer for the question that Isaac would eventually ask (Gen. 22:5–7)
      e.   Abraham saw God's promise, was assured of it, and embraced it. His trust in God and His promise was evident when he said his servants "we (not I) will come back to you" (Gen. 22:5) and to Isaac "God will provide for Himself a lamb for the burnt offering." (Gen. 22:8). Abraham stepped out in faith and used reason (not human reason, but reason to comprehend the character and promise of God), concluding that God was able (Heb. 11:19).

6.   Answers will vary.

7.   God is always able to deliver His people from their trials, but delivering every believer from every trial is not His will.

8.   a.   1.   Both Moses and his parents took specific steps of faith.
            2.   Bother Moses and his parents refused to let fear of Pharaoh's wrath keep them from living by faith (Heb. 11:23, 27).
      b.   Those who live by faith are able to *see* (comprehend, appropriate) God and His promises as realities.

9.   a.   They wanted a better resurrection—one that would be more honoring and pleasing to God.
      b.   A good testimony (NIV—"they were all commended for their faith").

10.   a.   Answers will vary.
       b.   Answers will vary.

Lesson 13 – *A Race Called Faith*

1.   a.   He must get rid of known sin in his life and everything that hinders his Christian walk and testimony.
     b.   1.   Jesus had to endure the excruciating agony of the Roman cross.
           2.   Jesus had to endure the shame of hanging naked before many onlookers.

2.   a.   Within the context, a weight refers to the loose outer clothing that would hinder the runners' performance. Here it is used metaphorically to refer to anything that might impede the believer's spiritual progress or witness. Sin, on the other hand, is the direct violation of God's Word.
     b.   Answers will vary.

3.   Believers need to keep their focus on Jesus Christ.

4.   a.   A Christian should examine his life carefully to see if there is any known sin in his life. He should give particular attention to those areas of his life in which he is experiencing trials. God's chastisement often comes in those areas of our lives where we are violating His Word (Gal. 6:7–8). If the believer examines his life carefully and finds he is not violating Scripture, he should assume it is a trial of faith and rejoice that he has been counted worthy to suffer for His sake (Phil. 1:29).
     b.   1.   God's chastening is proof that we are His children (Heb. 12:5–8).
           2.   God's chastening produces life (Heb. 12:9). Violating God's Word, on the other hand, is the way of death and destruction.
           3.   Believers become partakers of God's holiness (Heb.12:10).
           4.   God's chastening produces righteousness in those Christians who allow themselves to be trained by it (Heb. 12:11).

5.   a.   1.   Pursue peace (Heb. 12:14).
           2.   Pursue holiness (Heb. 12:15).
           3.   Be careful to live by God's grace and not let unforgiveness and bitterness live in your heart because it always infects others (Heb. 12:15).
           4.   Don't be involved with sexual sin (Heb. 12:16).
           5.   Don't regard the things of God lightly (Heb. 12:17).

6.   a.   The root (Greek—*pikria*) of bitterness is likely a reference to Deut. 29:18 and refers to anything that leads to idolatry and apostasy. A root is often below the surface, making it hard to detect. In the same way, the early forms of unforgiveness and bitterness can look like hurt or be masked as spiritual concern for the offender. A root is also the source of life for whatever grows. In the same way, a root of bitterness becomes the source of life for all sorts of sin (many are defiled). A root is often hard to destroy and unforgiveness and bitterness can be hard for a Christians to repent of unless they are fully committed to Christ's supremacy in their lives.
     b.   All Christians must learn to forgive others from their hearts.

    c.   God will deliver the unforgiving believer over to the torturers (Matt. 18:35). The Greek word for torturers (*basanistes*—torturers, jailors) indicates the punishment God inflicts on the unforgiving believer is equal to that which he (the believer) won't extend to the original offender. This torture continues until the unforgiving believer submits to God and forgives from the heart.

7.   a.   Esau, a skilled hunter (Gen. 25:27), came home from hunting, looking for something to eat. Jacob, his brother, bartered with Esau and gave him a bowl of stew in exchange for his birthright. Esau thought so little about his spiritual heritage that he sold it for a single meal.

    b.   Esau said, "Look, I am about to die; what is this birthright to me?"

Lesson 14 – *Changeless Christ, Timeless Truths*

1.   They were to show hospitability to strangers. Since there were few inns, showing hospitality to travelers was an important responsibility of the Christian's family life. Extending hospitality to strangers was a key element of the Jewish culture and this injunction was not supposed to cease now that the readers had been converted to Christ. The possibility of entertaining angels, as in the case of Abraham (Gen. 18:1ff.) and Lot (Gen. 19:1), should not be the primary motivation, but the potential of receiving an unexpected blessing should not be discounted. The Jewish believers were also to remember Christian prisoners (since you yourselves are in the body also). Prisoners were often mistreated and lacked daily necessities (food, warm clothing, cf. 2 Tim. 4:13) and often depended upon family and friends for these items. The writer wanted his readers to identify with the prisoners so their concern rose beyond sympathy to tangible expression of help.

2.   a.   1. Married people who commit adultery. 2. Spouses who make disparaging comments (jokes, sarcastic statements, etc.) about their mates. 3. Christians encouraging other believers to consider divorce on non-biblical grounds. 4. Christians who divorce for unscriptural reasons. 5. Christian men and women who fulfill their sexual desires independent of their spouse through pornography, fantasying, etc. Other answers could apply.

    b.   1. Love his/her spouse. 2. Remain morally pure in thought and conduct. 3. Train children to honor God in the area of marriage. 4. Stand up for the traditional definition of marriage as one man and one woman. 5. Support institutions such as schools, churches, etc. which uphold the traditional view of marriage. Other answers could apply.

3.   a.   God's judgment (Heb. 13:4). Poverty (Prov. 6:26). Severe damage to his own soul (Prov. 6:32). Wounds and dishonor (Prov. 6:33). Revenge from an enraged spouse (Prov. 6:34–35). Destruction (Prov. 7:26–27).

    b.   Answers will vary.

4.   True contentment is a gift from God to those who trust Him explicitly, acknowledge everything they have as a gift, and accept their rightful position as steward or manager

of everything He entrusts to them. The command to subdue the earth refers to fulfilling the God-ordained work that He has designed every person to accomplish—all in a spirit of trust and contentment.

5. 1.   They were to not forget their former spiritual leaders who had taught them God's Word or the spiritual influence they continued to have (Heb. 13:7)
   2.   They were to obey their spiritual leaders and manifest an attitude of submission to their spiritual authority for two reasons: 1. The spiritual leaders watch over our spiritual lives and give an account to God for how they lead. 2. Christians should want to be a blessing to the spiritual leaders rather than a grief.

6. a.   Jesus Christ's character never changes.
   b.   God's Word is true, His promises are real, His judgments are certain, His return is inevitable, and His saints are secure. Other answers could apply.

7. a.   Under the Old Covenant, the altar was the place upon which the sacrifices were offered. The writer isn't talking about a physical altar, for Christians have no sacred buildings or religious relics. The writer was referring to Jesus Christ, perhaps specifically the death of Christ on the cross, as the altar upon which He offered Himself for all sin. Christ is both the altar and the sacrifice.
   b.   The believer's body is the temple of the Holy Spirit.
   c.   The believer is to offer his life as a living sacrifice to God (Rom. 12:1). The believer should continually offer the sacrifice of praise to God (Heb. 13:15). The believer is to offer good works, including a readiness to share with others what God has entrusted to him (Heb. 13:16).

8.   Lord Jesus and great Shepherd of the sheep.

9.   Answers will vary.

10. Answers will vary.

THE FINAL EXAM

Every person will eventually stand before God in judgment — the final exam. The Bible says, ***And it is appointed for men to die once, but after this comes judgment*** *(Heb. 9:27).*

May I ask you a question? *If you died today, do you know for certain you would go to heaven?* I did not ask if you're religious or a church member, nor did I ask if you've had some encounter with God — a meaningful, spiritual experience. I didn't even ask if you believe in God, or angels, or if you're trying to live a good life. The question I *am* asking is this: *If you died today, do you know for certain you would go to heaven?*

When you die, you will stand alone before God in judgment. You'll either be saved for all eternity, or you will be separated from God for all eternity in what the Bible calls the lake of fire (Rom. 14:12; Rev. 20:11–15). Tragically, many religious people who believe in God are not going to be accepted by Him when they die.

> ***"Many will say to Me in that day, 'Lord, Lord, have we not prophesied in Your name, cast out demons in Your name, and done many wonders in Your name?' And then I will declare to them, 'I never knew you; depart from Me, you who practice lawlessness!'"*** *(Matt 7:22–23).*

God loves you and wants you to go to heaven (John 3:16; 2 Peter 3:9). If you are not sure where you'll spend eternity, you are not prepared to meet God. God wants you to know for certain that you will go to heaven.

> ***Behold, now is the accepted time; behold, now is the day of salvation*** *(2 Cor. 6:2).*

The words ***behold*** and ***now*** are repeated because God wants you to know that you can be saved today. You do not need to hear those terrible words, ***Depart from Me....*** Isn't that great news?

Jesus himself said, ***You must be born again*** (John 3:7). These aren't the words of a pastor, a church, or a particular denomination. They're the words of Jesus Christ himself. You *must* be born again (saved from eternal damnation) before you die; otherwise, it will be too late when you die! You can know for certain today that God will accept you into heaven when you die.

> ***These things I have written to you who believe in the name of the Son of God, that you may <u>know</u> that you have eternal life*** *(1 John 5:13).*

The phrase ***you may know*** means that you can know for certain before you die that you will go to heaven. To be born again, you must understand and accept four essential spiritual truths. These truths are right from the Bible, so you know you can trust them — they are not man-made religious traditions. Now, let's consider these four essential spiritual truths.

First Essential Spiritual Truth
The Bible teaches that you are a sinner and separated from God.

No one is righteous in God's eyes. To be righteous means to be totally without sin, not even a single act.

> *There is none righteous, no, not one; There is none who understands; There is none who seeks after God. They have all turned aside; They have together become unprofitable; There is none who does good, no, not one (Rom. 3:10–12).*

> *…for all have sinned and fall short of the glory of God (Rom. 3:23).*

Look at the words God uses to show that all men are sinners — *none, not one, all turned aside, not one.* God is making a point — all men are sinners. No man is good (perfectly without sin) in His sight. The reason is sin.

Have you ever lied, lusted, hated someone, stolen anything, or taken God's name in vain, even once? These are all sins. Just one sin makes you a sinner and unrighteous in God's eyes.

Are you willing to admit to God that you are a sinner? If so, then tell Him right now you have sinned. You can say the words in your heart or aloud — it doesn't matter, but be honest with God. Now check the box if you have just admitted you are a sinner.

❑ *God, I admit I am a sinner in Your eyes.*

Now, let's look at the second essential spiritual truth.

Second Essential Spiritual Truth
The Bible teaches that you cannot save yourself or earn your way to heaven.

Man's sin is a very serious problem in the eyes of God. Your sin separates you from God, both now and for all eternity — unless you are born again.

> *For the wages of sin is death (Rom. 6:23).*

> *And you He made alive, who were dead in trespasses and sins (Eph. 2:1).*

Wages are a payment a person earns by what he or she has done. Your sin has earned you the wages of death, which means separation from God. If you die never having been born again, you will be separated from God after death.

You cannot save yourself or purchase your entrance into heaven. The Bible says that man is **not redeemed with corruptible things like gold or silver** (1 Peter 1:18). If you own all the money in the world, you cannot buy your entrance into heaven. Neither can you buy your way into heaven with good works.

> **For by grace you have been saved through faith, and that not of yourselves; it is the gift of God, not of works lest anyone should boast** (Eph. 2:8–9).

The Bible says salvation is **not of yourselves.** It is **not of works, lest anyone should boast.** Salvation from eternal judgment cannot be earned by doing good works — it is a gift of God. There is nothing you can do to purchase your way into heaven because you are already unrighteous in God's eyes.

If you understand you cannot save yourself, then tell God right now that you are a sinner, separated from Him, and you cannot save yourself. Check the box below if you have just done that.

❑ *God, I admit that I am separated from You because of my sin. I realize that I cannot save myself.*

Now, let's look at the third essential spiritual truth.

THIRD ESSENTIAL SPIRITUAL TRUTH
THE BIBLE TEACHES THAT JESUS CHRIST DIED ON THE CROSS TO PAY THE COMPLETE PENALTY FOR YOUR SIN AND TO PURCHASE A PLACE IN HEAVEN FOR YOU.

Jesus Christ, the sinless Son of God, lived a perfect life, died on the cross, and rose from the dead to pay the penalty for your sin and purchase a place in heaven for you. He died on the cross on your behalf, in your place, as your substitute, so you do not have to go to hell. Jesus Christ is the only acceptable substitute for your sin.

> **For He [God, the Father] made Him [Jesus] who knew [committed] no sin to be sin for us, that we might become the righteousness of God in Him** (2 Cor. 5:21).

> **I [Jesus] am the way, the truth, and the life. No one comes to the Father except through Me** (John 14:6).

> **Nor is there salvation in any other, for there is no other name under heaven given among men by which we must be saved.** (Acts 4:12).

Jesus Christ is your only hope and means of salvation. Because you are a sinner, you cannot pay for your sins, but Jesus paid the penalty for your sins by dying on the cross in your place. Friend, there is salvation in no one else — not angels, not some religious leader, not even your religious good works. No religious act such as baptism, confirmation, or joining a church can save you. There is no other way, no other name that can save you.

Only Jesus Christ can save you. You must be saved by accepting Jesus Christ's substitutionary sacrifice for your sins, or you will be lost forever.

Do you see clearly that Jesus Christ is the only way to God in heaven? If you understand this truth, tell God that you understand, and check the box below.

❑ *God, I understand that Jesus Christ died to pay the penalty for my sin. I understand that His death on the cross was the only acceptable sacrifice for my sin.*

FOURTH ESSENTIAL SPIRITUAL TRUTH
BY FAITH, YOU MUST TRUST IN JESUS CHRIST ALONE FOR ETERNAL LIFE AND CALL UPON HIM TO BE YOUR SAVIOR AND LORD.

Many religious people admit they have sinned. They believe Jesus Christ died for the sins of the world but they are not saved. Why? Thousands of moral, religious people have never completely placed their faith in Jesus Christ *alone* for eternal life. They think they must believe in Jesus Christ as a real person and do good works to earn their way to heaven. They are not trusting Jesus Christ alone. To be saved, you must trust in Jesus Christ *alone* for eternal life. Look what the Bible teaches about trusting Jesus Christ alone for salvation:

> *<u>Believe</u> on the Lord Jesus Christ, and you will be saved (Acts 16:31).*

> *…that if you confess with your mouth the Lord Jesus and <u>believe</u> in your heart that God has raised Him from the dead, you will be saved. For with the heart one believes unto righteousness, and with the mouth confession is made unto salvation. For there is no distinction between Jew and Greek, for the same Lord over all is rich to all who call upon Him. For "Whoever calls on the name of the LORD shall be saved (Rom. 10:9–10, 12–13).*

Do you see what God is saying? To be saved or born again, you must trust Jesus Christ *alone* for eternal life. Jesus Christ paid for your complete salvation. Jesus said, *It is finished* (John 19:30). Jesus paid for your salvation completely when He shed His blood on the cross for your sin.

If you believe that God resurrected Jesus Christ (proving God's acceptance of Jesus as a worthy sacrifice for man's sin) and you are willing to confess Jesus Christ as your Savior and Lord (master of your life), you will be saved.

Friend, right now God is offering you the greatest gift in the world. God wants to give you the *gift* of eternal life, the *gift* of His complete forgiveness for all your sins, and the *gift* of His unconditional acceptance into heaven when you die. Will you accept His free gift now, right where you are?

Are you unsure how to receive the gift of eternal life? Let me help you. Do you remember that I said you needed to understand and accept four essential spiritual truths? First, you admitted you are a sinner. Second, you admitted you were separated from God because of your sin and you could not save yourself. Third, you realized that Jesus Christ is the only way to heaven — no other name can save you.

Now, you must trust that Jesus Christ died once and for all to save your lost soul. Just take God at His word — He will not lie to you! This is the kind of simple faith you need to be saved. If you would like to be saved right now, right where you are, offer this prayer of simple faith to God. Remember, the words must come from your heart.

> *God, I am a sinner and deserve to go to hell. Thank you Jesus for dying on the cross for me and for purchasing a place in heaven for me. I believe you are the Son of God and you are able to save me right now. Please forgive me for my sin and take me to heaven when I die. I invite you into my life as Savior and Lord and I trust you alone for eternal life. Thank you for giving me the gift of eternal life. Amen.*

If, in the best way you know how, you trusted Jesus Christ alone to save you, then God just saved you. He said in His Holy Word, *But as many as received Him, to them He gave the right to become the children of God.* (John 1:12). It's that simple. God just gave you the gift of eternal life by faith. You have just been born again according to the Bible.

You will not come into eternal judgment, and you will not perish in the lake of fire — you are saved forever! Read this verse carefully and let it sink into your heart.

> *Most assuredly, I say to you, he who hears My word and believes in Him who sent Me has everlasting life, and shall not come into judgment, but has passed from death into life (John 5:24).*

Now, let me ask you a few more questions.

According to God's Holy Word (John 5:24), not your feelings, what kind of life did God just give you? _____ What two words did God say at the beginning of the verse to assure you that He is not lying to you? _____ _____ Are you going to come into judgment? YES or NO _____. Have you passed from spiritual death into life? YES or NO _____.

Friend, you've just been born again. You just became a child of God.
We'd like to help you grow in your new Christian life. We will send you some Bible study materials to help you understand more about the Christian life. To receive these helpful materials free of charge, photocopy the form below, fill it out, and send it to us by mail, or you can e-mail your request to info@LamplightersUSA.org.

Lamplighters Response Card

❑ I just accepted Jesus Christ as my Savior and Lord on (date) _____, 20____ at
_____.

❑ I would like to begin attending a Bible-believing church. Please recommend some
Bible-believing churches in the area where I live.

❑ I already know of a good Bible-believing church that I will be attending to help me grow
as a new Christian.

Name _____

Address _____

City _____ State _____ Zip _____

E-mail
Address_____

Lamplighters International, 6301 Wayzata Blvd, St. Louis Park, Minnesota 55416, USA.

For additional Bible-Based, Christ-centered discipleship resources, including *Intentional Discipleship* seminars and on-line e-training

visit our website at www.LamplightersUSA.org

or contact

Lamplighters International, 6301 Wayzata Boulevard
St. Louis Park, Minnesota USA 55416

Toll-free 800.507.9516